THE RUSSIAN REVOLUTION, 1900–1927

Studies in European History

Series Editors: John Breuilly
Julian Jackson
Peter Wilson

Jeremy Black	*A Military Revolution? Military Change and European Society, 1550-1800*
T.C.W. Blanning	*The French Revolution: Class War or Culture Clash?* (2nd edn)
John Breuilly	*The Formation of the First German Nation-State, 1800-1871*
Peter Burke	*The Renaissance* (2nd edn)
Michael L. Dockrill and Michael F. Hopkins	*The Cold War 1945-1991* (2nd edn)
William Doyle	*The Ancien Régime* (2nd edn)
William Doyle	*Jansenism*
Andy Durgan	*The Spanish Civil War*
Geoffrey Ellis	*The Napoleonic Empire* (2nd edn)
Donald A. Filtzer	*The Krushchev Era*
Mary Fulbrook	*Interpretations of the Two Germanies, 1945–1990* (2nd edn)
Graeme Gill	*Stalinism* (2nd edn)
Hugh Gough	*The Terror in the French Revolution* (2nd edn)
John Henry	*The Scientific Revolution and the Origins of Modern Science* (3rd edn)
Stefan-Ludwig Hoffmann	*Civil Society, 1750–1914*
Henry Kamen	*Golden Age Spain* (2nd edn)
Richard Mackenney	*The City-State, 1500-1700*
Andrew Porter	*European Imperialism, 1860-1914*
Roy Porter	*The Enlightenment* (2nd edn)
Roger Price	*The Revolutions of 1848*
James Retallack	*Germany in the Age of Kaiser Wilhelm II*
Richard Sakwa	*Communism in Russia*
Geoffrey Scarre and John Callow	*Witchcraft and Magic in 16th- and 17th- Century Europe* (2nd edn)
R.W. Scribner and C. Scott Dixon	*The German Reformation* (2nd edn)
Robert Service	*The Russian Revolution, 1900-1927* (4th edn)
Jeremy Smith	*The Fall of Soviet Communism, 1985–1991*
David Stevenson	*The Outbreak of the First World War*
Peter H. Wilson	*The Holy Roman Empire, 1495-1806*
Oliver Zimmer	*Nationalism in Europe, 1890–1940*

Studies in European History
Series Standing Order ISBN 0–333–79365–X
(outside North America only)

You can receive future titles in this series as they are published by placing a standing order. Please contact your bookseller or, in case of difficulty, write to us at the address below with your name and address, the title of the series and the ISBN quoted above.

Customer Services Department, Macmillan Distribution Ltd
Houndmills, Basingstoke, Hampshire RG21 6XS, England

The Russian Revolution, 1900–1927

Fourth edition

Robert Service

First edition 1986
Second edition 1991
Third edition 1999

Fourth edition published 2009 by
PALGRAVE MACMILLAN

Palgrave Macmillan in the UK is an imprint of Macmillan Publishers Limited, registered in England, company number 785998, of Houndmills, Basingstoke, Hampshire RG21 6XS.

Palgrave Macmillan in the US is a division of St Martin's Press LLC, 175 Fifth Avenue, New York, NY 10010.

Palgrave Macmillan is the global academic imprint of the above companies and has companies and representatives throughout the world.

Palgrave® and Macmillan® are registered trademarks in the United States, the United Kingdom, Europe and other countries

ISBN-13: 978-0-230-22040-9   paperback
ISBN-10: 0-230-22040-1   paperback

This book is printed on paper suitable for recycling and made from fully managed and sustained forest sources. Logging, pulping and manufacturing processes are expected to conform to the environmental regulations of the country of origin.

A catalogue record for this book is available from the British Library.

A catalog record for this book is available from the Library of Congress.

10 9 8 7 6 5 4 3 2
18 17 16 15 14 13 12 11 10

Printed and bound in China

Contents

Contents

Editors' Preface

The Studies in European History series offers a guide to developments in a field of history that has become increasingly specialised with the sheer volume of new research and literature now produced. Each book has three main objectives. The primary purpose is to offer an informed assessment of opinion on a key episode or theme in European history. Second, each title presents a distinct interpretation and conclusions from someone who is closely involved with current debates in the field. Third, it provides students and teachers with a succinct introduction to the topic, with the essential information necessary to understand it and the literature being discussed. Equipped with an annotated bibliography and other aids to study, each book provides an ideal starting point to explore important events and processes that have shaped Europe's history to the present day.

Books in the series introduce students to historical approaches which in some cases are very new and which, in the normal course of things, would take many years to filter down to text-books. By presenting history's cutting edge, we hope that the series will demonstrate some of the excitement that historians, like scientists, feel as they work on the frontiers of their subject. The series also has an important contribution to make in publicising what historians are doing, and making it accessible to students and scholars in this and related disciplines.

JOHN BREUILLY
JULIAN JACKSON
PETER H. WILSON

Cartoons

Maps

Preface

When this book appeared in its first edition in 1986 it had two main objectives. Studies of the Russian Revolution had become uneven. Writers had been piling a mountain of attention upon the year 1917 whereas the decades on either side attracted only hillocks. By covering the period from 1900 to 1927, I wanted to make the case that the Revolution was best understood by broadening the chronological spectrum for investigation. At that time, too, the fashion was to write about politics, economics and society as if they were separate from each other. The pressing need was to put things back together. From the late 1980s, of course, much fresh information became available in the USSR when the Soviet communist leadership loosened its restrictions on access to documentary sources. The book's second edition incorporated such material; the third edition took account of the archival discoveries and historical discussion in the 1990s. This fourth edition retains the basic text, suitably smartened up, as well as the original structure and argument. The contents, though, have been modified in the light of further information and thought. The other change is the addition of a general introduction, which complements the preamble to each chapter. The Russian Revolution is as contentious in the early twenty-first century as it was when it happened. This is one thing about it that is not going to change.

I remain indebted to friends who generously suggested improvements to the first two editions: Roger Bartlett, Adele Biagi, John Channon, Olga Crisp, Bob Davies, Israel Getzler, Graeme Gill, the late Alan Hall, the late Jill Hall, Geoffrey Hosking, Evan Mawdsley,

Richard Overy, Arfon Rees and Steve Wheatcroft. For this fourth edition I have taken advice kindly offered by Simon Dixon, Julian Jackson, Julia Mannherz, Richard Ramage, Chris Read, Steve Smith, Jon Smele and Geoff Swain. My wife Adele Biagi has cast a critical eye on each successive edition and it is to her that I owe the deepest gratitude.

Technical vocabulary has been kept to a minimum and dates are given according to the calendar in official use at the time in Russia. A simplified version of the US Library of Congress transliteration code is followed; but well-known names like Trotsky, Witte and Zinoviev are given in their customary English form. As regards terminology, I have kept to the early twenty-century Russian definition of large factories as being those employing at least 16 workers with some motor-power or at least 30 without. A chronological table is appended with reference to the period covered by the book. References are cited in brackets according to the numbering in the bibliography, with page numbers being indicated by a colon after the bibliography number. A brief guide to the contents of general works on the Revolution is given in the bibliography's first section.

Robert Service

Introduction

The Russian Revolution set off a political earthquake. In February 1917 the Romanov monarchy tottered; in March it fell. This alone was an event of global significance. Russia and the other Allies were engaged in the Great War against the Central Powers. The Provisional Government, a shifting coalition of liberals and socialists, supplanted Emperor Nicholas II and its ministers proclaimed universal civil rights while assuming responsibility for national defence. They struggled to survive through months of political conflict and confusion. In October they succumbed to a seizure of power by Vladimir Lenin and the Bolsheviks. This second revolution was of still greater importance than the first. The Bolshevik party was dedicated to a more radical brand of socialism than any socialist minister in the Provisional Government had espoused – and the Bolsheviks for this reason were also beginning to call themselves communists in order to distinguish themselves from their more cautious rivals. Decades of agitation and organisation in Europe and North America had not yet given birth to a government composed exclusively of socialists. Bolsheviks in Russia saw themselves as the vanguard of the forces of revolutionary transformation.

If the action on Petrograd streets on 25 October had been all that happened, it would hardly have merited more than passing attention around the world. But within weeks the big industrial cities of the former Russian Empire were firmly in the hands of the Bolshevik-led government. Decrees were issued to turn the social order upside down. The 'transition to socialism' was announced and the Bolsheviks introduced a dictatorship to accomplish this. Hardly anyone abroad or even in Russia thought they would last for long in government. Not even the

1

Bolshevik leaders had high expectations from their revolution if they had to survive alone. They were hoping to be rescued by a 'European socialist revolution'. But although they won the Civil War which followed their seizure of power, they proved unable to spread the revolution to the rest of Europe. While consolidating their regime, furthermore, they had to recognise that Russian society and its economy could not be instantly transformed. But they took pride in the start they had made. They offered themselves as a model for ultra-leftist socialists everywhere to copy. They were building a new kind of society in the former empire. Theirs was a path towards a new and better modernity. 'History' was on their side.

This was the way that communists and their sympathisers looked at the Russian Revolution and its achievements [27: *28*]. Lenin was their hero. Even many people who saw blemishes in communist theory and practice went on judging the USSR on its own terms. They treated collective rights as deserving primacy over individualism and private financial profit. What good was political liberty if it did not guarantee the wide availability of food, health care, education and shelter? Generations of commentators, through to the collapse of communism in the USSR in 1989–1991, insisted that the Soviet order should be given the benefit of the doubt.

The case for the defence never obtained a majority verdict. From the first news of the October seizure of power there were politicians and journalists who thought Soviet Russia constituted a menace to world civilisation. The leading Russian liberal Pavel Milyukov denounced the Bolsheviks in such terms [51]. Winston Churchill referred to them as baboons. He called for Bolshevism to be strangled in its cradle and was disappointed when the Allies called off their military intervention in Russia and Ukraine. Some writers highlighted the disproportionate number of Jews in the Bolshevik party leadership. For them, the October Revolution was a Jewish conspiracy against Christian values – and this idea became the core of Adolf Hitler's Nazi ideology. Critics of the USSR subsequently suggested that the vast Gulag system of penal labour camps was no accidental development but the inevitable result of the installation of a regime committed to dictatorship and terror. Much as Soviet rulership changed, especially after Joseph Stalin's death in 1953, it was like an insect trapped in the amber of the ideology and practices of Lenin and the leaders of the Revolution in 1917. As such it was unreformable: it had to be entirely eliminated.

A range of analyses of the Russian Revolution stood between the extremities of endorsement and rejection. One early suggestion was that the Bolshevik party had introduced a bastard version of European socialism heavily conditioned by the specificity of the Russian environment. Austrian Marxist Otto Bauer welcomed it, however resignedly, in these terms [40]. Menshevik leader Yuli Martov and German Marxist writer Karl Kautsky agreed with such a description, seeing the Soviet regime as the combined product of a backward popular culture and malevolent intellectual leadership. Yet far from accepting the Soviet regime, they urged the need for a campaign to moderate and civilise it [48; 50]. They agreed, though, that the Bolsheviks were socialists of some kind or other. Not all socialists went along with this. Many denied that Bolshevism, with its zeal for political dictatorship, had anything to do with the essence of socialism. In their eyes, the Bolsheviks had damaged the socialist reputation worldwide. Not surprisingly this led to confusing wrangles. The Bolsheviks insisted on calling themselves socialists as well as communists; their socialist enemies challenged their entitlement to represent socialism in the slightest fashion.

Another turn of analysis came from Nikolai Berdyaev, who proposed that the USSR was basically not a new, socialist order but the latest mutation of Old Russia. Instead of a tsar, it had Lenin. Instead of Orthodox Christianity it had Marxism. And it retained the mechanisms of oppression well known in the Russian past [41]. A concurrent strain of such thinking was offered by Nikolai Trubetskoi and the self-styled Eurasianists. Their idea was that Russia had always been a hybrid of Europe and Asia; they concluded that Berdyaev was naïve to call on the Bolsheviks to be more moderate. Trubetskoi believed harsh methods of rule were essential to the country's territorial security and political stability [59].

Foreigners joined in the debate after visiting Russia. Bertrand Russell and H. G. Wells went out to Moscow in 1920; they came back depressed by the Bolshevik propensity for violence but impressed by the party's sincerity of purpose [54; 61]. There were also several travellers who believed that Bolshevism in theory and

3

practice was a living nightmare [46]. Others like John Reed and Max Eastman were generous to the Bolsheviks [47; 53], and assessments of a kindly sort gained prominence from the early 1930s as the Soviet achievement in mass education and industrial growth made a positive impression worldwide. The USSR was touted as an archetype of 'modernisation' capable of being used elsewhere around the globe. Walter Duranty, Sidney and Beatrice Webb and George Bernard Shaw supplied admiring eyewitness reports [31: *203–7*]. They vouched for Stalin's credentials as democrat and champion of justice. They praised his economic record and condoned his arrest and killing of opponents. They also followed him in tracing Stalinist policies to the nature of the state established by Lenin and the Bolsheviks in the October Revolution. Russian émigrés had already supplied a variant of this kind of interpretation. The 'Change of Landmarks' group, headed by Nikolai Ustryalov from his émigré base in northern China, argued that the Bolshevik party deserved credit for regathering the Russian lands and reimposing order – and Ustryalov contended that the groundwork had been laid for economic advance as communists sloughed off their ideology and prioritised the traditional interests of state [60].

Professional scholars produced little in the way of deep empirical study of the Russian Revolution before the Second World War. Historians in the USSR were subject to state censorship. They were barred from raising difficult questions about the working class; some of them in the 1920s did, however, publish insightful work on the peasantry [154]. Even abroad the scholarly record was flimsy. Just a few exceptions existed. The Carnegie Foundation funded pioneering studies by emigrants about Russia in the First World War but not about the Revolution itself [283]. The British communist academic Maurice Dobb wrote the first substantial work of Soviet economic history, which covered the decade after the October seizure of power [99].

Most of the detailed chronicles came from outside the academy. American reporter W. H. Chamberlin put together an impressive account of the revolutionary years [43]. The other serious works were written by leading participants in the politics of 1917. They belonged to the legion of the defeated: the Mensheviks, the Socialist-Revolutionaries, the Constitutional-Democrats and Lev Trotsky. They explored their memories and the documentary collections available to them as refugees or deportees in the West, and the result was a bank of writings from which it was possible for later generations to draw even if they did not subscribe to a similar political philosophy. Thus it came about that Trotsky, a communist leader thrown out of the USSR by Stalin, could gain wide acceptance for his argument that the difficulties of communism in Russia derived from the economic and cultural backwardness inherited from the Russian Empire. He also argued that an anti-revolutionary, bureaucratic stratum of officials led by Stalin had secured control of the Soviet order by the mid-1920s [58]. The Mensheviks said all along that all the Bolshevik leaders, including Trotsky himself, had contributed decisively to the disappointments in the path-breaking attempt to build a society of harmony and affluence in the USSR [45; 57]. Trotsky, though, sold more books and his interpretation made a more lasting imprint on opinion in the West about the reasons for the failure of the communist leadership to attain all its revolutionary ends.

It was only after the Second World War that Western writers got into their stride. They were an assorted bunch. On the political left were Isaac Deutscher and E. H. Carr who approved of the early Soviet regime to a greater or lesser extent [6; 9]. These two were opposed by Leonard Schapiro and Merle Fainsod who believed the October Revolution was an unmitigated disaster for the human race [10; 30]. As the Cold War intensified, governments financed the creation of research institutes for Russian studies likely to demonstrate the iniquities of Soviet communism. The dominant idea was that Lenin and his Bolsheviks had invented doctrines and methods of total control which were adopted not only by the new communist parties but also by the extreme political right, especially by Hitler and the Third Reich. This same idea was the hub for theories of totalitarianism.

The rancour between left and right disguised the fact that both sides agreed that high politics were the motor of all changes in the Russian Empire and the USSR. Kremlin leaders and policies preoccupied attention through to the 1970s. This was when a younger generation of historians began to question whether it was sufficient to focus on high politics in accounting for how things turned out in the wider state and society. Fresh kinds of analysis came to the fore: 'history from below' and 'social history'. The number of studies mushroomed. Ronald Suny examined the non-Russians [253]. The present author investigated the Bolshevik party in the localities [245]. Diane Koenker and Stephen Smith studied the factory workers of Petrograd and Moscow in 1917 [162; 258]. Orlando Figes probed the Volga peasantry. The focus was on constructing a wider framework for historical research than had been offered by the early post-war writings. Around this time there was also an effort to show that a more humanitarian version of communism might have emerged at the end of the 1920s if only Lev Trotsky or perhaps – as Moshe Lewin and Stephen Cohen suggested – Nikolai Bukharin, instead of Joseph Stalin, had won the struggle to succeed Lenin, who died in 1924 [7; 21]. This was a more traditional approach, being centred on high politics; and in the instance of Trotsky it involved a reversion to the analysis already offered by Deutscher.

The newer writing became known as 'revisionist'. It soon became clear that its practitioners agreed about little besides the need to expand the frame of analysis. Controversy was focussed on political questions while society, culture, economics and international relations stayed free from fundamental dispute. And although there was nothing like consensus about politics under Nicholas II and the Provisional Government, it was the communist advance on power and the establishment of the Soviet regime which gained the lion's share of attention. There were two poles of general analysis. Sheila Fitzpatrick gave no room for the Bolsheviks as manipulators of the minds of their working-class supporters. She also treated the dictatorial practices of the early communist regime as largely the consequence of unpredicted difficulties encountered after the October Revolution [12]. Meanwhile Richard Pipes, who repudiated 'revisionism' in all its forms, saw the Bolsheviks as having acted wholly malevolently. For him, Lenin all along intended to impose a one-party terror state and had only contempt for the workers [26]. Between these poles there were several accounts, including this one, generally suggesting that an understanding of the Russian Revolution required the blending of 'high politics' of the Bolsheviks and the social and cultural setting [11; 29; 36].

Not until the collapse of the USSR at the end of 1991 could historians in Russia enter the discussion with complete freedom, and several of them picked up the interpretation developed dec-ades earlier by the totalitarianist school of commentary. This was a school that retained support among many Western scholars [23; 26]. Vladimir Buldakov stood out against the trend in Russia, arguing that the Revolution was better interpreted as one of the country's 'times of troubles' [4].

Research has proliferated as archives have been opened for examination in the countries of the former Soviet Union. The First World War has attracted overdue research. Particular cit-ies and regions in the revolutionary period have come under scrutiny. Broad cultural and social processes have begun to be surveyed. The result is that the chronicle of the Russian Revolu-tion is now accessible in its day-by-day minutiae. But consensus about causes, process and outcome remains elusive. Innovative ways of analysing the sources have been proposed, including post-modernism. It has been suggested that both the post-war writers and even many of their revisionist successors had a politi-cal preoccupation which lessened their capacity to appreciate the sheer diversity and contradictions of the revolutionary experi-ence [265]. The opposing viewpoint has been that the October Revolution is incomprehensible unless politics are kept in sharp focus; indeed the argument has been put forward that many revi-sionists unjustifiably downplayed the significance of high politics [191; 245: *157–62*; 239; 264; 275].

The discussion continues. The Russian Revolution was one of the formative events of recent world history. It had an imme-diate, deep impact which lasted through to the Second World War and beyond. The USSR until 1945 was the world's sole com-munist state (except for its puppet administration in Mongolia). The October 1917 seizure of power encouraged the creation of Marxist-Leninist parties in Europe, north America and elsewhere. The wish to prevent the spread of Soviet communism had an influence on the establishment of fascist and right-wing authori-tarian governments. The USSR, against the odds, defeated the Third Reich in the Second World War. Communism was trium-phant, suddenly expanding into eastern Europe and China and eventually covering a quarter of the world's land surface. The new communist states, despite their national variations, imitated the Soviet order to a great extent in their policies, institutions and doctrines. The Cold War, starting in the late 1940s, involved a global struggle between two great coalitions of powers headed by the USSR and the US. World peace was under threat through to the end of the 1980s when President Ronald Reagan and General Secretary Mikhail Gorbachëv brought their countries to terms with each other. For decades until its dissolution in 1991 the Soviet order, born in October 1917, influenced politics in every continent.

This book summarises the abundant literature on the Russian Revolution while offering an interpretation of its own. Its stress has always been on the need to pull together all kinds of history – political, social, economic, cultural and international. The general line can be briefly stated. The revisionists were right to broaden the scope of factors explaining the outcome of the October Revolution; their critics were equally correct in insisting that Bolshevik doctrines and policies were always highly authoritarian.

What is more, the purposes and acts of the communist party leadership directed, conditioned or impinged on nearly every aspect of life in Russia after the Bolshevik seizure of power. Politics, especially high politics, mattered immensely. Yet the constraints on the central communist leadership were constantly severe. Communists had expected to preside over an easy process of revolutionary consolidation. Instead they found themselves ruling a society where many fundamental patterns of belief, custom and aspiration were against them. Their early attempts to force themselves on 'the people' proved impractical, and they were obliged to adjust their doctrines. Although they had invented a new kind of state – the one-party, one-ideology state – they still had to make compromises. By the end of the 1920s, though, they had become acutely impatient with their situation. Despite their willingness to adapt to circumstances, they remained committed to an ideology of total transformation. Their isolation in the world and even in their own society reinforced an eagerness to get on with the process.

This was not just Joseph Stalin's personal mood but also corresponded to the feelings of most veterans of the party which had overturned the Provisional Government. The way was clear for what became known as Stalinism. There was no inevitability about Stalin's emergence as despotic leader. But the institutions, practices and philosophy needed for that outcome were inscribed in the history of communism before Stalin mounted to supreme power. Stalinism was a bastard product of Leninism. Lenin would have disowned it, no doubt, but he could never have convincingly denied paternity.

Map 1   The Russian Empire in 1900 © Robert Service

O C E A N

PACIFIC
OCEAN

R. Lena

Okhotsk

Yakutsk

Sakhalin Island

Krasnoyarsk

Lake Baikal

Irkutsk

Vladivostok

JAPAN

KOREA

C H I N E S E   E M P I R E

Map 2   The USSR in 1927 © Robert Service

OCEAN

PACIFIC
OCEAN

R. Lena

Yakutsk

SOCIALIST REPUBLIC (RFSR)

Krasnoyarsk

Lake Baikal

Irkutsk

Vladivostok

MONGOLIAN PEOPLE'S REPUBLIC

KOREA

JAPAN

CHINA

1 Unstable Structure, 1900–1914

Why did the Russian Imperial monarchy crumble to the ground in February 1917? Communist historians in the USSR used to maintain that it was a collapse waiting to happen and that Lenin and his Bolsheviks delivered the decisive last push [27; 28]. Most writers other than communists rejected this general line. They disliked any such kind of historical determinism; they were also sceptical that the Bolshevik contribution to the downfall of the Romanovs was of much influence. They did agree, though, that the Russian Empire had basic problems. Travellers to Russia before 1917 emphasised how unmodernised the country was and how backward and oppressive the conditions of the lower social orders were. The Imperial order had the reputation of being the 'prison of the peoples' and the fortress against democracy and enlightenment in Europe. Revolution was only to be expected in such circumstances.

Not everyone in the West accepted this gloomy summary. The economic and educational record of tsarism was not unimpressive, and many commentators suggested that the economy would have gone on progressing if the Russian Empire had not entered the First World War. Thus a rise towards the level of contemporary advanced capitalism has been seen as a genuine possibility [15]. There has also been a degree of support for the politics of tsarism. Nicholas II, widely despised and detested in his time, has recently been described as an intelligent, flexible leader [178]; and some Western and Russian historians have argued that the overthrow of the Romanov monarchy was the result of an unpatriotic betrayal by every political grouping – not just by Lenin's Bolsheviks but by other socialists as well as liberals and conservatives [37]. Furthermore, it has been emphasised that the sequence of diplomatic clashes between Russia and its foreign rivals before

1914 was not predestined to end in military conflict [22]. Things could have turned out differently. Writers of this persuasion conclude that the Russian Empire was sound enough, politically and economically, to have survived if the war had been avoided. No war, no revolution.

Such accounts have not convinced most analysts. The conventional opinion has been that a revolution of some kind, if not unpreventable, was highly likely. Every aspect of the Romanov order gave signs of weakness. Nicholas II was unvisionary and unbending. The political system was underpinned by a police state and by arbitrary rule [26; 292]. Whole social classes as well as entire national and religious groups resented the status quo. Poverty was widespread and was aggravated by an industrial drive that neglected rudimentary popular needs. The Russian Empire was a powder keg waiting to explode.

Many recent historical works, however, have highlighted the unprepossessing situation which was Nicholas II's inheritance. Their argument runs as follows. The tsars ruled over the world's largest land-based empire and therefore had extremely long borders to defend. Rival powers existed to the west, the south and the east. Military imperatives constricted the revenues left over for social and economic reform. So did the need to hold the peasants back from revolt and to maintain the obedience of the non-Russians. The administrative network had gaping holes and the police were under-resourced. Transport and communications were thinly spread. The industrial lead achieved by North American and European economies was large and growing larger [72]. Meanwhile most Russians had a sense of nationhood linked to their tsar and their Orthodox Christian faith, but their primary identity was associated with their family and their village [17]. There was nothing at all near to consensus about a common national purpose and the antipathy towards the upper and middle social classes was wide and deep. Many intellectuals too were alienated from the regime. This set of circumstances, it is suggested, would have put the capacities of any conceivable Russian government to an extreme test in the early twentieth century. Thus although Nicholas II was hardly an outstanding emperor, it was the general situation and not his personality that enfeebled the regime's reaction to the assaults made upon it. The overthrow of the Romanovs grew likelier as year succeeded year.

The gathering storm, some have maintained, came from the social consequences of over-rapid industrialisation. There is much in this. Most people suffered material hardship and social injustice. But there were also positive aspects to the economic transformation. A section of the working class and peasantry benefited from the expansion of industry and commerce. Moreover, the tsarist state was nowhere as repressive towards national and ethnic minorities as was Stalin's later despotism. Indeed several writers have proposed that tsarism was rendered vulnerable not so much by the ravages of industrialisation as by the continued vigour of traditional social units – the peasant communes, the religious sects, the factory work gangs – which hated and undermined the political order whenever the chance arose. And arise it did for a while in 1905–1906 and then with devastating effect in February 1917 [34].

The explanation advanced in this chapter is that the Russian Empire, before the First World War, had to deal with a double crisis: a crisis produced by hostile forces of assertive modernity and a crisis produced by the enraged forces of ancient custom. The Imperial order might – just about might – have resolved one or other crisis in isolation; but the two of them together produced an explosive situation. The Romanov monarchy and its administration could not adequately constrain and conciliate the 'modern' elements in society. Nor could it enforce its will upon the old, traditional elements. It was steadily losing in both contests. Furthermore, the empire's various weaknesses – political, economic, ethnic, social and cultural – were tightly interlinked and systemic. Of course, a sense of proportion is necessary here. The empire as it was developing by 1914 was a sensitive plant, but it was not doomed to undergo the root-and-branch revolution of 1917. What made that kind of revolution possible was the protracted, disruptive, exhausting conflict of the First World War. No First World War, no October Revolution. Lenin and his Bolsheviks were donated a revolutionary opportunity they would probably never have created for themselves.

[i] St Petersburg and the world in 1900

Let us go back to 1900. Many contemporary observers took it as axiomatic that Nicholas II's removal from power would enable

16

the solution of all the country's political, social and economic problems. Yet these problems were not surmountable solely by a change of regime. Looked at from St Petersburg, the world outside the Imperial borders had never seemed more threatening. Peace in Europe was brittle. Two great powers, France and Prussia, had gone to war against each other in 1870. Germany, after its unification under Prussian leadership in the same year, rose to dominance in the politics and trade of the continent's central regions; and its ally, Austria–Hungary, strove to expand its own influence in the Balkans. The quest for security encouraged Russia to sign an alliance with France in 1894 as a counterweight to German power in Europe. But Germany also posed a challenge in Persia and the Near East especially after the Germans signed commercial and military agreements with the Ottoman Empire. Diplomatic crises recurred. In the Far East, meanwhile, Japan effected rapid industrialisation and became yet another regional rival to Russia. This was the era of imperialist aggrandisement. China was the largest prey, and Russia extracted consent that northern China lay within its sphere of control. Russian imperialism had a long history. Ukrainian, Siberian, Baltic, Polish and Caucasian lands had been conquered. As recently as the 1870s, the army had been sent to subjugate areas in central Asia; and with the Ottoman Empire on the brink of dissolution, ministers in St Petersburg aspired to acquire the Straits of the Dardanelles.

This was a dangerously fluid situation. Tensions were increasing among the great powers and complacency was not in order. Any government in Russia wishing to prevent domination by foreign states or even territorial dismemberment had to stimulate the kind of economic and cultural transformation that had brought international success to Britain, France, Germany and the US. The use of steam power and, latterly, electricity in factories had transformed whole economies. The armed forces of industrialised countries acquired a massive technical advantage, and their educational facilities provided training in the mental skills newly necessary in every walk of life. Having undertaken the project of modernising the country later than its competitors, the Russian regime was under more acute pressure to accomplish it. The problem was not unique. Countries like Italy and Spain had faced it, and others in Africa, Asia and South America confront it to this day.

Yet Russia had other predicaments which made her unique in Europe. The climate was extremely unhelpful. Vast tracts of Siberia lie over permafrost, and huge parts of central Asia are deserts. Russia proper had more clement weather. But winter in St Petersburg and Moscow is much longer than in London, Paris and New York. Soil quality left a lot to be desired across the empire. Only limited areas, principally in the southern Ukraine and the southern steppes, approached the fertility of North America's cereal-growing belts. The empire's sheer expanse too was another burden. It is 5000 miles from eastern Poland, which was then administered directly from St Petersburg, to Vladivostok on the Pacific coast; and 2000 miles stretch between Murmansk in the frozen Russian north and the Turkish frontier. The domain of the Russian emperor dwarfed the landmass of every other state. Canada, the US and China were small by comparison. Transport across the empire met with huge obstacles. It was a very unfortunate accident of geography that the great navigable rivers flowed away from the main economic centres. The dispersal of raw materials was an additional drawback. Gold and timber had come from Siberia and oil came from Baku by the Caspian Sea. Although St Petersburg had become the focal site for the metal-processing industries, the great deposits of coal and iron were hundreds of miles away in the Donets Basin. Ethnic diversity was a further complication. Russians constituted only two-fifths of their land-based empire's population. Poles, Latvians, Ukrainians and Azeris had regional majorities in places vital to the country's industrial health.

Russia's transformation could therefore not fail to be arduous. Economic backwardness meant that the country had to make fundamental changes very fast in order to compete with the advanced capitalist powers, and this was bound to unsettle a social order already in perilous flux. And both climate and topography pushed the financial costs higher than were encountered abroad.

[ii]   The Romanov monarchy before 1905

Strong state power was needed, as elsewhere, to compel the labour force to forgo any drastic improvement of its living standards;

УПРАВЛЯЮТЪ НАШИМИ ДЕНЬГАМИ

МОЛЯТСЯ ЗА НАСЪ

ѢДЯТЪ ЗА НАСЪ

СТРѢЛЯЮТЪ ВЪ НАСЪ

МЫ РАБОТАЕМЪ НА НИХЪ, А ОНИ —

Cartoon 1 A satirical pre-1914 cartoon about the structure of power in the Imperial monarchy. The comments, from top to bottom, are as follows:

'They dispose of our money.'
'They pray on our behalf.'
'They eat on our behalf.'
'They shoot at us.'
'We labour for them while they …'

firm direction was also required to co-ordinate the economy's advance. The Imperial state was headed by an absolute monarchy. The Romanov dynasty had ruled since 1613, and no emperor in the nineteenth century permitted the election of a national representative assembly. Political parties were banned. Public meetings were strictly supervised and a pre-publication press censorship was applied. Rebellion was rare. Regicide occurred in 1762 and 1801, but these were coups that replaced one dynastic incumbent with another. Even the unsuccessful popular revolt raised in 1773 by Emelyan Pugachëv against Catherine II lacked a definite commitment to basic social reform. Not until 1825 was a truly revolutionary organisation formed. This took shape as a conspiracy of army officers and other nobles; and 'it was easily crushed. Nicholas I, who was crowned in 1826, retained massive authority for himself and his successor Alexander II. A personal cult of the emperor was encouraged, and it was largely effective: peasants cherished the icon of the ruler which they pinned to their hut walls. Moreover, the emperor's word was law, quite literally. Any oral instruction from him could overrule legislative enactments. Monarchical whim was pervasive. The Council of Ministers bore little resemblance to a British cabinet: it held no collective deliberations and every minister was held responsible to the monarch alone [298: *21–2*]. The crown also appointed the governors who directed the organs of provincial government. Such appointees were invested with huge powers; and the police in the localities had the right to mete out punishments by administrative fiat. The Russian Empire was not just a police-state; it was also a state of extremely arbitrary rule [292: *4*].

Whether this structure was fit to deal with the tasks being undertaken by the empire at the end of the nineteenth century is doubtful. But unqualified dismissal would be anachronistic. It was still in the not so distant past, in 1789, that France's absolute monarchy had been dismantled. In addition, parliamentary democracy was cramped even in the UK; the British franchise was extended to all male adults only in 1884. Repression of anti-establishment groups persisted even longer elsewhere. The German social democrats remained outlawed until 1890. In the US, some employers got away with violent persecution of socialists well after the 1920s. The Russian monarchy was an extreme case of authoritarianism in a world that had many grades of unfreedom.

Nevertheless the rulers became deeply aware of the need for economic transformation after recognising the inadequacies of the Russian military effort in the Crimean War against Britain and France in 1854–1856. Alexander III, mounting the throne in 1881, proved himself a consistent industrialiser. So did his son Nicholas II, who acceded in 1894. Neither was intellectually inspired or inspiring. But their support for industrial growth was solid. Sergei Witte, Minister of Finance from 1892 to 1903, appreciated the uses of autocracy in this connection. A Russian parliament elected through a universal adult franchise would have turned the peasantry's demographic predominance into political influence. The resultant preferences might have included a lowering of taxation and, in financial policy, a heightening of indulgences for the sector producing agricultural equipment. Even if the peasants had failed to get their demands satisfied in full, the effect might still have been damaging to investment in armaments. Perhaps the same difficulties would not have arisen if the autocracy had granted a franchise restricted to the propertied classes. This had been the pattern of German modernisation, and the Japanese employed it successfully in the 1890s. But industrialists were proportionately fewer in Russia; and the Russian landed nobility contained a larger body of opinion hostile to prioritising industrialisation: emulation of Germany would have created its own problems. Witte and others concluded that a resolute autocrat in St Petersburg could play a helpful role in stimulating and protecting industrialisation. Alexander III and Nicholas II did so and the urban middle class made progress under their shelter.

Every state has internal divisions. The Ministry of Internal Affairs, being aware of the risks of pushing the peasantry too hard, warned repeatedly against fast industrial expansion [233: *417–18*]. Other institutions were less obstructive. The Russian Orthodox Church acted loyally as the government's power spiritual. But the ignorance of priests was legendary, and such efforts as were made to renovate the ecclesiastical hierarchy and its policies gave no assistance to the drive for economic and cultural modernisation [98: *340–7*]. Thousands of officials in the civil bureaucracy also were apathetic or simply bemused. Venality was endemic. Nepotism and inefficiency were an Imperial shame. At the same time, though, ministerial competition for resources was intense. The standing army was a drain on the exchequer; its duty to complete the subjugation of the Caucasus and hold down eastern Poland was costly. But the Ministry of Finance acquitted itself well in the struggle over the budget. The entire regime was in the grip of transition. The state administration was not just a form of exclusive indoor relief for hereditary nobles who had failed at farming. On the contrary, four-fifths of posts in the highest four grades of the civil service before the First World War were held by men who were not landed gentry; and non-nobles had become a majority in the army officer corps by 1912 [179: *401*].

[iii] Economic progress

The government's handling of industry was robustly positive. State ownership and state contracts contributed vitally to capitalist economic development in Russia. The possession of weapon-producing factories had been a traditional objective of the authorities; but the railways too were recognised for their importance: two-thirds of the network in 1914 were state property. Increased revenues were obviously necessary. The myth persists that industrialisation was achieved through a universal impoverishment of the peasantry. In fact the largest portion of the government's income, 40 per cent in 1913, came from customs and excise duties – and if people had not been able to pay the tax on salt and vodka the state budget would have been in ruinous mess [93: *4*]. Central direct taxes were comparatively low; even Witte, hardly the peasant's friend, treated an expansion of rural purchasing capacity as indispensable. The government in any event could not finance development solely from its own coffers. Less than a ninth of the industrial capital stock was in its hands at the outbreak of the First World War [90: *51–2*]. Domestic private enterprise was nurtured. The 'monster tariff' of 1891 gave protection to Russian manufacturing; it also stimulated foreign companies to set up branches inside the empire whereas earlier they had exported to Russia. The decision of 1897 to put the rouble on the gold standard attracted further investment from abroad. It is estimated that foreigners owned 47 per cent of Russian securities, excluding mortgage bonds, by 1914 [90: *154*].

There were dangers in relying so heavily upon injections of capital from western Europe in an international environment that was anything but tranquil. Witte recognised this but astutely predicted that a massive withdrawal of funds would not occur. Russian creditworthiness was excellent: profits were solid even though they were never as great as Witte's propagandists promised since maladministration and poor transport wiped out the advantages of gaining a low-wage work force. French and Belgian finance led the way in boosting activity on the St Petersburg stock exchange. The empire's strategic interests were being well served, and the course of Russian industrial development was not deflected by foreign economic pressures. Russia was not Bulgaria. Her government was not so easily intimidated.

Yet the world trade cycle was beyond her control, and the Russian Imperial economy remained vulnerable to the periodic recessions in the rest of Europe. The slump between 1900 and 1903 was especially damaging. Yet the country also benefited from Europe's booms, so that by 1914 the empire was the fifth largest industrial power on earth. The growth rates were imposing. Industrial output expanded annually by 8 per cent in the 1890s and by 6 per cent between 1907 and the beginning of the Great War [126: *149*]. Railway construction began in earnest in the 1860s. Some 30,000 miles of track were laid in the pre-war period and the Trans-Siberian line was completed in 1916. Russia became the world's fourth greatest producer of coal, pig iron and steel. Oil extraction was highly successful: only Texas rivalled the Baku fields. Naturally areas of weakness remained: the chemical, electrical and machine-tool industries gave chronic cause for concern [112: *12*]. Even so, factories in Russia were starting to turn out lathes, locomotives and motor cars. Capital goods of this sort were anyway not the only sector of endeavour. Mass consumer demands increased throughout society. Textiles continued to be Russia's biggest single industry through to the First World War; and together with food-processing they supplied 50 per cent of total industrial output value whereas the figure was 14 per cent for mining and metallurgy [90: *34–5*]. The balance between capital and consumer products in industrial output was not particularly unusual for a country at Russia's stage of modernisation [134: *430*].

The suggestion that industrial advance was achieved at the cost of agricultural regression remains unproved. Russian agrarian indices point to a moderate advance. The harvests of wheat and rye, which were the mainstay of Imperial agriculture, increased in the second half of the nineteenth century [206: *284*]. A famine afflicted the Volga region in 1891–1892. Climate could play havoc with even the best-organised farms [291: *27–8*]. Yet improvement, despite intermittent setbacks, was solid. Grain output rose by an annual average of 2 per cent between 1881 and 1913 in European Russia (or by 1.1 million tons per annum) [290: *3*]. Dairy products were finding their way to markets in Germany where Russian yoghurt was much admired. The Imperial economy was definitely not all guns and no butter.

The regime's disparagers passed over this achievement in silence. They focused on the negative aspects. The Imperial population increased steeply in the second half of the nineteenth century with the result that the benefit of the agricultural expansion was less than it would have been. Even so, per capita cereal production in European Russia went on rising, possibly by as much as 35 per cent from 1890 to 1913 [149: *270*]. The Empire became the largest cereal exporter in the world and ports on the Black Sea like Odessa were turned into bustling commercial entrepôts. In the half-decade before the First World War, merchants in Russia and Ukraine sold abroad an annual average of 11.5 million tons [290: *2*]. Imperial agriculture was also beginning to diversify. Trade in potatoes and dairy products gained in commercial significance, especially from Poland and the Baltic. Meanwhile Ukraine, southern Russia, the Urals and western Siberia achieved their huge expansion in wheat output. Sugar beet too emerged as an important crop; the area given over to it, chiefly in Ukraine, rose by 38 per cent in the decade before the Great War [102: *225*]. Nor were industrial crops ignored. Cotton growing was taken to Turkestan as the Russian elites sought to exploit their recently conquered areas. The prospect of further rural economic progress in the Russian Empire was growing ever stronger. Sales of agricultural machines and other equipment increased. Investment in such stock appears to have risen at an annual rate of 9 per cent from 1891 to 1913 [136: *274*].

[iv]   The transforming of Imperial society

Yet the modernisation of both industry and agriculture had a long, long way to go. St Petersburg was a majestic, modern city with buildings, theatres and parks which earned the admiration of visitors from abroad; and Moscow, Odessa, Warsaw and Kiev were not far behind in global renown. Change, though, was geographically patchy. The citadels of advanced economic performance and cultural attainment were surrounded by vast tracts of habitation where little had altered in centuries. Few cities were anything like miniature versions of the Russian capital. And tens of thousands of villages, especially those which were distant from railway lines, slumbered on unacquainted with novel techniques of production.

The government's financial policies as well as its orders for railways and armaments aided industrial growth. It was less solicitous about agriculture. Peasants felt they were being left to fend for themselves. Certainly the Land Bank established for them in 1882 merely scratched the surface of their problems. And not even the government's defenders claimed that its encouragement of industry was comprehensive. Aside from sectors of recognised strategic importance, Russian enterprises were expected to operate without state assistance. Lobbying of ministers was not a highly developed art. In any case, ministerial bureaucracies were not the sole agents of economic charge. Social forces supplied massive momentum. Indeed the spurt of officially fostered industrialisation in the 1880s and 1890s was preceded by decades when state policies had been inimical in some ways to industrialism as such. The entrepreneurial spirit of Moscow factory owners was famous. Jewish financial and commercial effervescence was moving across the western borderlands. Armenians were shaking up the trading patterns in the south Caucasus.

In the nineteenth century the regime placed limits on the pace of change. In particular, it preserved the peasant land commune. Rural lads had to seek permission from the village elders to leave for work in the towns. Such a stipulation reflected the government's wish to curtail the enlargement of the landless poor. It used to be thought that the desire was fulfilled. After all, there were only 3.1 million workers in factories and mines in 1913. But the working class included other groups too. The addition of railwaymen, builders, waiters, home-based workers and domestic servants yielded a total of 15 million (and 20 million if agricultural wage-labourers were taken into account) [228: *329, 333*]. This was a fourfold increase over 1860.

The growing industries required a growth in the provision of basic schooling. The government wished to expand educational and social amenities in order to emulate the great powers in Europe. From 1864 it allowed the election of organs of rural self-government – each being known as a *zemstvo* – with limited responsibilities for schools, roads and hospitals; and the existing municipal councils were allowed to fulfil similar local tasks. Central government itself put a vast school-building programme in hand. Nearly two-thirds of all factory workers in European Russia, according to a survey in 1918, were literate; and, in metropolitan printing and metal-processing plants, reading and writing accomplishments were well-nigh universal [228: *601*]. The Russian worker's similarity to his counterpart in Germany or Britain should not be overstated. Most members of the industrial workforce kept in touch with their native villages and many held on to their plots of land [171: *139*]. Working-class life was pretty rough. Fist fights and hooliganism were endemic, especially among people who were newly arrived from the countryside and living in poverty [83; 201]. Social change obviously had a long way to go. But it was happening. Russia was acquiring an ever-larger 'hereditary working class', schooled in basic literacy and numeracy and trained to operate complex machinery.

Although the villages left behind by these workers changed less than the towns, they were not unchanging. Emperor Alexander II had issued the Emancipation Edict in 1861. Until then the peasantry, which constituted nine-tenths of the population, was either legally tied in personal bondage to the owners of the land where they were born or else consisted of state peasants under the tutelage of governmental officials. The nobility and the Imperial family were the country's greatest private landowners. Their peasants, while being emancipated as persons, received an unfavourable economic settlement. The average amount of land obtained by them across the empire, excluding Poland, was 13 per cent less than they had previously cultivated. In the more fertile regions such as in southern Russia, the nobility made the peasants forgo a third or even a half of what they had previously tilled [125: *730*].

Matters did not stand still at that. The total terrain held as property by nobles proceeded to diminish. Sell-ups became a stampede after 1905. It is reckoned that the nobility had owned twice as much land in the 1860s as it managed to retain by 1912. Absentee landlords were also on the increase and many estates were rented out. Townspeople were among those who took over the noble estates, but most of the new owners and tenants were former serfs. The peasantry's share in the agricultural economy, far from being compressed, achieved a remarkable growth. Buying and renting of land occurred on a massive scale. Close to nine-tenths of European Russia's sown area by 1916 was under cultivation by peasants [169: *182*]. It is reckoned that 87 per cent of the total value of the empire's agricultural output between 1909 and 1913 was produced by them [169: *190*]. The expansion of a market economy inevitably eroded age-old village customs. So did the spread of literacy as Alexander II followed up the Emancipation Edict with a series of educational and administrative reforms in the 1860s. Although progress was understandably slower than in the towns, a survey of a dozen provinces in European Russia before the Great War revealed that about two-fifths of the male rural population had learnt at least how to read and write their own names [229: *294*]. Evidently life in the countryside was not yet transformed; but the achievement was not trivial and the drive towards new styles of existence appeared irreversible.

Not all nobles went bankrupt before they left the land. Many departed simply because they were offered outrageously good prices or because jobs in the civil service or even business beckoned [168: *124–6*]. Owners of large landed estates in southern Ukraine and in the Baltic region, furthermore, became successful rural capitalists [203: *29*]. The gentry marketed twice as large a proportion of its harvest as the peasants did of theirs [169: *188*].

The incentive for such a social group in countryside or city to seek political reform was small. There were several reasons for this. Business was generally healthy in most years as the economy expanded. Moreover, the various sections of the propertied elite were distracted by rivalries. Noble landowners defended their interests against the industrial bourgeoisie and in 1898 secured a weakening of the tariff system which protected the growth of factories in Russia. Dues payable on imports of agricultural machinery were scrapped. There was also a successful campaign, guided by the Minister of Internal Affairs V. K. Pleve, to dissuade the emperor from sanctioning a proposal to confer noble status upon distinguished non-noble figures in trade and industry [168: *151–2*; 261: *301–3*]. Yet industrialists and bankers, whether or not they hailed from lowly backgrounds, could count their blessings. The state, with its contracts and its help when the work force went on strike, was too valuable in defending the commanding heights of the urban capitalist economy for them to strain after its overthrow; and there was more huff and puff in the grievances of rural capitalists than genuine bite. The Ministry of Finance had arranged the railway freight rates so as to make it cheap for farmers to reach markets for their produce inside and outside the country. Imperial Russia was a playground for the rich whether they wore the boots of landowners or the town shoes of bankers and industrialists [156: *173–4*].

[v] Social discontents

Yet with the development of the working class in the towns there came a multitude of problems. Most Russian factory workers were poor. Many were earning only enough for subsistence and were subjected to harsh, humiliating treatment at work. Safety regulations were widely ignored. Foremen could fine labourers for minor or even imaginary infringements of rules. The average working day, without overtime, was between 12 and 14 hours in the 1880s [161: *42, 47*]. Housing was bad. For the majority the choice lay between gloomy company barracks and costly, unhygienic, overcrowded rented rooms. Health care was abysmal. Social insurance, where it existed at all, was extremely expensive.

These conditions do a lot to explain the rebelliousness that turned the Russian working class into a worldwide legend in 1905 and 1917. The squalor was not unique to Russia. Although sections of the industrial workforce in countries like Britain and Germany were beginning to enjoy a somewhat more comfortable life by the turn of the century, even western Europe contained areas of dreadful misery. Most workers in Milan and Turin were little better off than those in St Petersburg – and the spirit of revolt flourished equally in all three cities. In any case not all Russian labourers were political rebels. It was once thought that the trouble came mostly from the unskilled 'raw youths' from the countryside who swarmed into the towns and occasionally formed unruly mobs. But this failed to account for the quiescence of Irish immigrants to Birmingham. It is evident from Russian industrial conflicts, moreover, that the leadership and inspiration came from the more skilled and more urbanised sections of the workforce [77: *210*]. As elsewhere, such workers tended to have the understanding and the organisation to take up the struggle for better treatment. A slight rise in average real wages occurred between 1900 and 1913 and it was most remarkable among the skilled trades [89: *407*]. But it was the slightness of the improvement and not the improvement itself that most workers noticed.

Poor conditions and rising expectations produced turbulence in Britain, France and Germany in this period. The same was true in the Russian Empire. Strikes were not spectacularly large before the turn of the century; the year 1899 was the peak year of the decade for industrial conflict, when the number of the strikers was only 97,000 [167: *225*]. But the continuing ban on trade unions aggravated tension. This was recognised in all the main industrial countries, albeit only eventually and often with reservations, except Russia. The rapidity of industrialisation made it vital to open channels for the expression of grievances; and the gigantic size of many factories in Russia intensified the sense of a gulf between employers and employed. Two-fifths of workers in industrial firms belonged to workforces of over 1000 in 1914 [156: 7].

The peasants, apart from some disturbances in the early 1860s and late 1870s, did not put the police to much bother in the last century. Yet their basic unhappiness was of an acute kind. They were angry that so much of the land they cultivated had to be rented from gentry landowners, who were also hated for hanging on to crucial pastures and woods. This largely detracted from any rise in the income accruing to the peasantry. In any case, the rise was an aggregate figure that disguised the gradations of living standards. Most peasants in European Russia lived in communes. The government used this institution as a cost-free tax-gathering and self-policing facility. Communes in central and northern Russia periodically redistributed their land among resident peasant households. But inequalities persisted so that the more affluent peasants, known as kulaks, hired other peasants as labourers or became money-lenders. The village poor in Russia, as in Ireland and Germany [185: *138*], lived in piteously poor conditions. This focused rural minds on the land question. Peasant land-hunger was almost universal and the belief that noble landowners should be constrained to give up their land was deeply held. Then there were the discriminatory laws. Peasants, until 1904, were subject to corporal punishment for misdemeanours. The post of 'land captains', who were charged with keeping order in the villages and who often were from the gentry, was a further vexation.

[vi]   Political upheaval: 1905–1906

The possibility that the discontent might turn into political opposition was the government's nightmare in the late nineteenth century. Enlightened labour laws were passed. But implementation was patchy, and the army was used to break up strikes. Wage battles between employers and employees automatically acquired a political significance. Workers increasingly discerned this. So too did students. The officious university deans, the mandatory uniforms and the niggardly financial support annoyed them. Postgraduate unemployment was a further irritation [217: *45–6*]. It is true that the bureaucracy gave jobs to numerous ex-students, and that state enterprises like the railways were major employers. But a ponderous insistence upon hierarchy and routine was resented by a frustrated young generation through to the end of the regime. Some entrenched themselves in the 'free professions' like law and medicine. Others made their mark in the zemstvos [110: *426–8*].

Many intellectuals believed that the absolute monarchy was the primordial cause of the country's ills. Clandestine organisations were formed from the 1860s onwards aiming to rebuild society on the foundations of egalitarian traditions in the peasant land commune. The militants by focusing upon 'the people' earned their description as 'populists' (*narodniki*). Their passionate argument was that a transition directly to a socialist order was practicable. A party, Land and Freedom, operated in the 1870s and recruited hundreds of peasants. But the vast rural majority never knew its name. Land and Freedom's propaganda had little effect; and the assassination of Emperor Alexander II by its terrorist offshoot, People's Freedom, caused revulsion in 1881. Yet an estimated 5000 revolutionaries resumed activity in the political 'underground' in the ensuing two decades [204: *42*]. The populists came to recognise that capitalism was planting deep roots in the Imperial economy; they also saw that the urban working class was more responsive than the bafflingly quiescent peasantry to political slogans. Secret trade unions were formed at the risk of arrest by the workers from 1874 onwards. Political liberty was among their demands. Populists strove to enter and direct such organisations. From the 1880s they were rivalled by groupings which adapted the doctrines of German Marxism to conditions in Russia. The Russian Marxists extolled the advantages of urbanism and large-scale social units; in their estimation, a bourgeois-led republican government had to be established before there could be a campaign for a further transition to socialism. Their strategy won more supporters than populism in the late 1890s. But linkage with the mass labour movement was attained only fitfully. The political police, known as the Okhrana, rounded up activists in hundreds. Liberals were harassed; the neo-populists, the Socialist-Revolutionaries, suffered prison and exile. The Marxists, whose 10,000 adherents made them the largest anti-monarchist party in 1904, were hunted hard [241: 25].

Repression by itself did not work well enough for the government and other preventive measures were tried. The legislation discriminating against the peasantry began to be repealed after the turn of the century. Attention was directed at the workers too. A few trade unions were legalised, but they were saddled with harsh restrictions and kept under surveillance by the Okhrana. Quickly this experiment was adjudged dangerous by the Ministry of Internal Affairs and was under threat by 1904.

The remnants of one such union in St Petersburg, led by Orthodox Church priest Father Georgi Gapon, induced upheaval in the following year. Rostov-on-Don, which had been in tumult in 1902, had had to be pacified militarily. St Petersburg three years later was less easily controlled. On 9 January 1905, guards units fired upon Gapon's peaceful procession in favour of constitutional and social reforms. 'Bloody Sunday' provoked strikes and public marches. The non-Russians went to the fore in defying the government as Poles set up barricades in cities and Georgia virtually became self-ruling. The Finns too were restless. The armed forces, moreover, had been preoccupied by a disastrous war with Japan since 1904 and hundreds of mutinies followed the defeats in the Far East [84: 86]. Workers in Russia and elsewhere created their own unofficial councils by election. The Russian word for council is soviet. These soviets, quickly evolving beyond

31

the functions of strike leadership, set up apparatuses of local administration. Political revolution loomed. Peasants, their harvest ruined by drought, were restive. Illegal pasturing and wood felling on gentry land occurred in the summer, and agricultural wage-labourers went on strike [108: 96]. Cases of arson increased. Occasional seizures of land occurred. Village communes, wherever they existed, helped to co-ordinate the anti-gentry revolt. A Peasants' Union was established. But the rebels in the countryside acted independently of the Union: it was in the towns that large organisations of any kind made an impact. Men, not surprisingly in view of the Russian family's traditions, took a bigger part than

Cartoon 2   M. M. Chemodanov's cartoon from 1905, depicting the rabbit attacking the bear after the lion has killed the bear. The lion is the 'proletariat', the bear is the tsarist regime and the rabbit is 'the liberal bourgeoisie'.

women [132: *81–2*]. Trade unions were formed even among civil servants, waiters and the unemployed. Factory workers were not alone on the streets. Industrialists doubted the government's technical competence and joined the initial clamour for a constitution.

The monarch's fate hung by a thread as political parties emerged from the shadows. Mutiny erupted in the Black Sea fleet. The Marxist leadership of the Moscow Soviet mounted an armed uprising of workers in December 1905. Emperor, ministers, high command and police were widely reviled. Newspapers across nearly the entire spectrum of public life carried editorials predicting fundamental change in the Russian Empire.

[vii] The limits of the regime's adaptiveness

Two things saved the regime: its unsparing use of the army and its last-ditch promise of political concessions in the October Manifesto of 1905. All the revolts were quelled or deflected. A parliament, or State *Duma*, was promised. It duly met in April 1906. The Duma's powers were very restricted since it could neither appoint ministers nor pass laws autonomously. It was also liable to dissolution at the emperor's behest. And yet a chastened Nicholas II was willing to display favour towards leaders of Russian liberalism. He invited a few liberals, including Pavel Milyukov, into the Council of Ministers. This political semi-compromise was not a Russian invention; it was the kind of idea practised in Germany through to 1918. But the offer came too late for impatient, overconfident liberals in the Russian Empire – and perhaps it would even have been a difficult trick to pull off earlier. At any rate the liberals, who had formed the Constitutional-Democratic Party (or Kadets), spurned the proposal and held out for a parliament with independent legislative authority. In the First Duma they spent their time haranguing ministers. To their horror, Nicholas II issued a decree to disband the proceedings. The monarch and his premier Pëtr Stolypin were no more enamoured of the Second Duma; and in 1907, by means of something like a coup d'état, they revised the electoral rules so that the landed gentry might dominate the new chamber. This resulted in the Third State Duma. The Duma's largest party were reform-minded conservatives known as the Octobrists, who accepted the new limits of legal political behaviour and aimed to gain an influence over the government by co-operating with it in the Duma.

Stolypin wanted to avoid relying too heavily upon the rural nobility. He therefore sought to strengthen the peasantry's rights in the local elections to the zemstvos [145: *155*]. This attempt was frustrated. It ran athwart the nobility's interests, and Nicholas II acceded to requests to maintain the status quo. Noble landowners set their face against sharing their rural dominance even with neighbouring industrialists [190: *369–70*]. Stolypin's ambitions anyway had inner contradictions. It was he who had arranged to prevent the peasantry's demographic strength from being duly registered in the Third Duma. He had also ordered the execution of the peasant 'ringleaders' of 1905. Field courts-martial summarily sent 2694 such men and women to their death [106: *448*].

In 1911 Stolypin himself was killed by an assassin; but his political fortunes had long been in eclipse. Nicholas II was his empire's greatest landowner and remained reluctant to go against the wishes of the landowning class. The emperor had never been keen about constitutional reform, and courtiers never failed to voice their concerns about Stolypin's innovations [284: *129–34*]. Steadily the will to preserve his dynasty's powers intact ruled over other desires. In 1909 he took offence at Stolypin's proposal that, in order to keep sound relations with the Octobrists, the Duma should be permitted to vet matters such as the Imperial navy's budget. Nicholas and his wife sought out advisers they found more congenial. They welcomed quacks and the 'holy man' Rasputin in their court. Ministerial office became ever more closely associated with bribery and corruption. Forthright crown servants like Witte and Stolypin gave way to toadies. Although a few courtiers made criticisms of the trends in public life, they castigated the symptoms of decadence and not the disease: they reviled Rasputin while refusing to recognise more basic political problems. Furthermore, the quasi-constitutional settlement of 1906 involved an Imperial State Council as a counterweight to the far from weighty Duma. The State Council was drawn from the higher spheres of state, Church, zemstvos, business and landed nobility, and its conservative majority regularly upset initiatives for change emanating both from the Duma and from Stolypin

[106: *491*]. This suited the instincts of Nicholas II, whose nominations to the State Council reflected his rigidity.

Russian nationalism was fast becoming the regime's last standby. Shadowy associations arose on the political far right. Among them were the Black Hundreds which carried out pogroms against Jewish communities in the name of God, Holy Russia and the tsar. The central government, while disapproving of such lawlessness, lacked the will and enough police to put a stop to it [162: *24, 33–4*; 173: *205, 207, 233*]. Traditional chauvinism also took non-violent forms. The Orthodox Church, the ecclesiastical arm of government, displayed its creativity mainly by heightening its intolerance towards the other Christian denominations and the Moslems. Meanwhile the Ministry of Foreign Affairs asserted Russia's role as protector of the Slavs in the Balkans.

[viii]   Social resilience and institutional growth

Yet the monarchy's power was on the wane. It is true that the revolutionaries were spectacularly defeated and crushed after 1905. For instance, the adherents of organised Marxism – the Russian Social-Democratic Workers Party – fell numerically from 150,000 in 1907 to 10,000 in 1910 [109: *36–7*]. But the power of the Imperial government was much more effective in brief, intense trials of strength than in perennial political struggle. The police state was still only half-built. Indeed the Russian Empire had seven times fewer policemen as a ratio of the total population than the UK [238: *56*]. To be sure, this comparison can be a misleading one inasmuch as it takes account neither of the garrison troops deployed to keep order nor of village 'self-policing' by peasants. Nevertheless the control of civil society became more problematic after 1905 when the weakness of state authority had been exposed. It was hard enough to keep tabs on political activities. It was harder still to regulate the spread of ideas, especially after 1906 when the censorship ceased to require publishers to submit manuscripts before publication. Not that successive censors were outstandingly perceptive. Marx's *Das Kapital* had appeared legally in translation in 1872. The roll of honour of Russian literature, furthermore, includes authors from Alexander Pushkin through to Lev Tolstoi and Maxim

Gorki who evaded the ban on their works by dressing up their political criticisms in indirect language. The terminology became still less restrained before the First World War. Editors were still prosecuted and their presses closed down by the authorities, but even the revolutionary parties managed to resume publication: usually they simply renamed their newspapers and continued printing as previously.

Not all the technological innovations that facilitated the extremely repressive states headed by Stalin in the Soviet Union and Hitler in Germany had yet been disseminated. Nicholas II's government anyway did not envisage such excesses of regimentation as an objective. The executions of 1906–1909 were more the exception than the norm. Exile was the usual punishment for political dissenters, but many of them suffered badly from the climate and isolation in northern Russia and Siberia [295: *23*].

Even so, the regime's efforts to mobilise popular favour behind it were diminutive. They could even be counterproductive. The coronation of Nicholas II in 1896 was planned so poorly that hundreds of onlookers on Khodynka Field were trampled to death. State occasions, such as the celebration of the Romanov dynasty's tercentenary in 1913, were subsequently better arranged; and sums were assigned for publications depicting the emperor as working selflessly for the good for the people [296: *457, 487*]. But governing circles in St Petersburg lacked the imaginativeness of their counterparts in Berlin or London in developing new rituals and propaganda to elicit a renewed consent from society. The Russian monarch, moreover, ruled an empire of mutually hostile nations, and Russians constituted only 45 per cent of his subjects. It was very difficult to obtain the approval of most Poles and many Finns without allowing them to secede from the empire. The Ukrainians and Belorussians, who as Slavs were ethnically close to the Russians, were not so implacable; and, in the south Caucasus, the Georgians and Armenians knew that independence would expose them to the threat of a Turkish invasion [248: *665–70*]. But the Imperial authorities did little to enhance their reputation among non-Russians. Chances to rally backing from Russians were also overlooked. Nicholas II, like his predecessors, thought more about the interests of empire than about nation building. Most

Russians were peasants and their vision of life was circumscribed by the concerns of village, agriculture and Christian festivals; they knew little about anything beyond the limits of their own little village. Once upon a time the authorities had found this very convenient. If peasants were to have acquired a deeper understanding of Russia and the world, they might have become a national force that disturbed the Imperial equilibrium.

The middle classes made scant effort to integrate the Russian lower social classes into a wider sense of society. They usually disdained to found the football clubs and choral societies that fostered civic pride and, to some extent, an inter-class culture in the West [237: *36, 39*]. Probably social antagonisms were too unyielding for cultural integration to have been successful. The divisions between the propertied few and the impoverished millions were sharp and deep. Social welfare was meanly provided. Admittedly the zemstvos founded schools and hospitals, but the resultant tax burden was resented by peasants; and a small number of 'people's houses' were privately established in the big cities to supply workers with reading clubs [146: *77–8*]. All in all, though, endeavours of philanthropic nature were insubstantial.

So working men were insulated from the state and the middle classes. They therefore organised their own groupings. From the mid-nineteenth century they were forming Sunday schools. These were devoted to initiating or broadening the education of the adult pupils, and they attracted revolutionaries as volunteer teachers. Another point of activity was the sickness-insurance funds, even though by law they had to include employers' representatives. Taverns were favourite gathering spots. The growth of both atheism and alcoholism caused much official anxiety; but labourers befuddled by vodka were not a threat to the regime. Other modes of social intercourse were much more disturbing. The government was worried about the groups of workers linked by common geographical origins and known as *zemlyachestva*. In these, a man could relax and talk with little fear of being overheard by the police. The October 1905 Manifesto, furthermore, led to a proliferation of still larger organisations in the form of trade unions. Admittedly about 600 unions were shut down by 1911. But some always survived, and their leaderships trained hundreds of working-class functionaries to handle their affairs. The co-operative movement flourished and thousands of agricultural co-ops existed by 1914 [152: *14*]. These also encountered bureaucratic harassment, but the effect was only to increase the alienation of their largely peasant membership from the political status quo. Independent social organisations, despite governmental interference, were a fact of life. 'Autocratic Russia' was no longer in a traditionally autocratic fashion.

[ix]   Economic problems before 1914

Even before 1905 the government had seen agrarian reform as its last hope of survival. The rural turbulence in that year convinced official and landowning opinion that the peasant commune, far from acting as a prop for the existing order of things, undermined the foundations. Communal agriculture was associated with three-field crop rotation with the division of each field into several strips for each household and, in European Russia, with periodic redistribution of land among households. Russian peasant agriculture, for all its advances, remained backward by the standards of the Western great powers. Stolypin's wish, when he became premier in 1906, was for the peasants to disband the commune, to consolidate a household's strips of land into a contiguous holding and to hand property deeds to the heads of household. Independent, prosperous smallholders were his goal.

In fact, only about a tenth of peasant households in the empire's European zone consolidated by 1916 [103: *572, 583*]. The government had made the terms of exodus from the commune increasingly easy. Even so, the fall of individual applications to leave after 1909 was never reversed. The warmest welcome for agrarian reform occurred in the fertile south of the Russian Empire. But the average size of consolidated farms set up in three Ukrainian provinces to the west of the river Dnieper was nevertheless hardly massive: just 15 acres [103: *586*]. Most peasants anyway preferred the commune's guarantee of collective welfare, however inadequate, to the uncertainties of individual farming. In fact the Ministry of Agriculture relented its anti-communal drive before the Great War. It was finding that the 'consolidators' were often the most blatant exponents of soil-exhaustive methods because the pressure on them to make a quick profit was intense. By contrast, many communes were eager for advice on the introduction of multifield crop rotations [209: *441, 445*]. The problem was that action through the commune involved settling for a lengthy schedule for agricultural progress. Meanwhile, the climate was still ruining the harvest about once every seven years. The poor soil quality in northern Russia meant that the region had to import grain and potatoes to subsist; and central Russia, which had traditionally exported its surplus northwards in the previous century, failed to increase its output before the First World War as fast as the rise in its population [290: *6–7*].

Imperial agriculture, then, was poised precariously between painstakingly won success and occasional disaster. The run of good harvests from 1909 to 1913 concealed the problems. Russian industry faced dilemmas. The trough of 1905 and the ensuing recession was followed by sustained recovery aided vitally by an enormous French loan; and expansion continued through to the First World War. But again the appearance of advance, with the non-state civilian economy at last breaking entirely clear of its past reliance upon state support, is deceptive.

Governmental projects remained important in Imperial industrial production. After the defeat in the Russo-Japanese war of 1904–1905, when the Baltic fleet was annihilated, metallurgy received a boost from vast defence orders [123: *105–7*]. The priority given to 'rearmament' was scarcely unique to Russia; but Germany, Britain and France were at a more advanced stage of industrialism. The deflection of investment away from civilian objectives had more adverse effects upon Russia, whose transport network needed to be denser than it was. The St Petersburg government, furthermore, nurtured a cosy relationship with a small number of huge firms. Delivery on time and at fixed prices was thought to suit the state's interest better than laissez-faire competition. Scandals of excessive profits recurred [176: *138*]. It was unfortunate that these same metallurgical companies could not satisfy the demand for agricultural implements. Imports of tools and machinery, particularly from the US, expanded. Many firms not blessed with governmental contracts found the going hard. Although the Russian Empire's industrial output increased before 1914, the still higher rate of expansion in the US and Germany meant that the gap in productive capacity was widening [72: *1104, 1108*].

[x] Political instability

Yet the economy's achievements must not be understated. The dynamism of Russian agriculture and industry was impressive, and the strictly economic difficulties, in the factories if not in the countryside, posed no immediate threat to capitalist development. But the poverty of most workers and peasants remained. Its persistence was a Damoclean sword dangling over Imperial politics.

The ultimate emergency drew nearer as factory labourers returned to the offensive. In 1912, 2032 strikes broke out. The timing of the outburst was affected by the boom which had increased opportunities for employment and allayed the fear of confronting employers; and the long-standing grievances of working people had been made more acute by the changes introduced into factories to raise labour productivity after 1905 [143: *171*]. The emphasis on 'scientific management' was not merely a bosses' offensive even though this was undoubtedly part of the story. Wages were low by the standards of advanced industrial economies; but labour overhead costs, as measured in the provision of housing and training, were much higher [89: *404*]. The pressure on industrialists to rationalise their operations was severe. Any lingering doubts about the government's involvement on the bourgeoisie's side vanished with the shooting of striking workers in the Lena gold fields in April 1912 – sympathy with the labour movement spread far and wide in reaction to the massacre [190: *154–7, 193*]. The crescendo continued. In the first half of 1914 alone there were over 3000 strikes, and two-thirds of them were associated with political demands. Many strikers were demanding a democratic republic, an eight-hour working day and the expropriation of gentry-held land [138: *365*]. These were slogans espoused by the more radical of the Marxists such as the sympathisers of Vladimir Lenin and Lev Trotski [278: *191*]. The Okhrana's penetration of revolutionary groupings remained deep and successful; and few workers were acquainted with Marxist doctrine. Yet as social unrest increased, huge demonstrations against the monarchy were organised in St Petersburg in summer 1914. These were suppressed and a revolutionary situation was pre-empted, but the fragility of the political order had been exposed yet again [188: *315–7*].

Court and government appeared incompetent and distasteful to an ever-larger segment of the middle classes. Nicholas II succumbed to autocratic recidivism. The base of his support became gravely narrow when, in 1913, Alexander Guchkov and other Octobrists made overtures for an anti-governmental pact with the Kadets. Thus did moderate conservatism announce its despair of winning the emperor's sympathy. On the other hand, the monarchy's self-professed friends outside the Duma, such as the Union of the Russian People, urged a comprehensive programme of repression and anti-constitutionalism that was manifestly outside the regime's powers to realise.

Events abroad superimposed themselves upon the political disarray in St Petersburg. On 28 June 1914 the Austrian Archduke Franz Ferdinand was assassinated in Sarajevo, and the Habsburg government in Vienna held the Serbian government responsible. Russia announced its support for the Serbs. When Austria-Hungary, encouraged by the German government, declared war on Serbia, the Russian emperor ordered his army's general mobilisation. The Germany high command gained the pretext it wanted to defeat the Russians before they became even stronger. On 1 August, as St Petersburg refused to stand down its forces, Berlin declared war on Russia. The German war plan called for an attack on France over the plains of Belgium. The UK, which had signed a guarantee of Belgian neutrality, was pulled into the diplomatic proceedings, and on 4 August the British cabinet issued an ultimatum for the Germans to evacuate Belgium. No reply was forthcoming from Berlin. The Great War had begun. Although its first battles were fought in Europe, it had ramifications throughout the world. Two great coalitions confronted each other. The Central Powers were headed by Germany and Austria-Hungary and the Allies by France, Russia and the UK.

The motives of each government were complex and controversial. In Russia, it was Nicholas II who took the crucial decision to fight. His patience with both Austria and Germany was exhausted. He was striving to preserve his country's prestige and her pretension to status as a Great Power. His upbringing and outlook inclined him to the military option in summer 1914. Also of influence on him was the course of international relations in recent years. Around the turn of the century, St Petersburg and Berlin had settled their rivalries without much difficulty. But Russia drew closer to her French ally after 1905 when loans raised in Paris saved the Imperial regime. Germany's frustrations about her own global position grew in the same period. A Franco-German dispute over Morocco in 1905–1906 resulted in Berlin's diplomatic defeat. But then Germany successfully sustained Austria-Hungary's annexation of Bosnia in 1908 in the teeth of the remonstrations of Serbia. Russia had spoken in Serbia's favour, but the risk of war with Germany intimidated Nicholas II into climbing down. In 1914 he was unwilling to suffer another such humiliation [22].

Probably he would have been goaded into a declaration of war even if he had not declared it voluntarily. Conservative and liberal politicians in the Duma were equally alert to questions of Imperial 'honour' and material interest [181: 69]. Economic as well as geopolitical issues were at stake. German industrial penetration of Russian markets was deepening. Many magnates of Russian industry, banking and commerce looked forward to asserting themselves over a vanquished Germany and desired Russia annex the Straits of the Dardanelles.

Nicholas II and his trusted advisers also calculated that a short, victorious war would quieten the tremors of revolution at home. The stress in official pronouncements was placed on patriotic duty. War hysteria quickly gripped the country and the danger of defeat was hardly discussed. The emperor's action was widely applauded. Worker and owner, peasant and landlord, civil servant, lawyer and aristocrat: all sections of Imperial society joined in the military enthusiasm. Plans for anti-governmental strikes and demonstrations were abandoned. Governmental optimism was in the ascendant, and certainly the Russian Imperial armed forces were not so dreadfully ill-prepared as was once supposed; indeed the German high command had been fearful that Russian power would become insuperable unless a pre-emptive war were waged. But the first campaign in eastern Prussia was a massive setback for Russia. At the battle of Tannenberg, in August 1914, the German forces encircled the Russians and took hundreds of thousands of prisoners. A rapid strategic retreat took place and the Imperial Army dug trenches and prepared to resist Germany's first offensive. It became clear that the war would be a protracted one. And the strains of all-out, lengthy warfare were bound to tell harder and harder on the Russian Empire's economy and society. The point of political explosion was moving nearer.

2 Demolition, 1915–1917

How did it come about that the Bolsheviks could seize power in the Russian capital in October 1917? Their success, according to Soviet spokesmen over many decades, resulted from the close fit between the party's policies and the aspirations of the workers, peasants and conscripts of the former Russian Empire. They claimed that socialist revolution was unavoidable and that the military, economic and political disarray of wartime Russia was a mere backdrop for the doom of capitalism; at the same time they asserted that the role played by Vladimir Lenin was vital to the revolutionary advance [27; 28]. This picture of the leader, the party and the 'masses' acting in benign harmony has always been rejected by non-communists. But about one thing there was agreement: the importance of Lenin. Practically everyone in the West at the time and later concurred that without him there would have been no October Revolution. His indispensability was treated as axiomatic.

Everything else about the official Soviet interpretation was rejected. Some works maintained that Lenin and the Bolshevik party had always distrusted the working class and that in 1917 they systematically misled popular opinion in quest of political power [26]. Why Lenin might have done this remains controversial. His detractors see him as a megalomaniac interested only in naked power. Others suggest he believed in the working class before he held power and changed his mind only later [141]. Aside from this discordance, there has been concurrence that the battle for revolutionary Russia was between one political elite and the others: the Bolshevik party versus the other socialists. Workers, soldiers and peasants did not act independently. Soviets, trade unions and other organisations were dominated by political elites, and the only difference between the Bolsheviks and their opponents was in the level of doctrinal fanaticism, tactical cunning and internal obedience shown by each side. And no one could match Lenin in willpower and intuition. By its sustained cultivation of the popular mood, the Bolshevik party rose from obscurity in February 1917 to a position where it could head a further revolution in October [19].

Yet while interpretations differed, the basic descriptions were similar in West and East. Apparently it was all very simple: Lenin dominated the party, and the party dominated the masses. Of course, the USSR's spokesmen claimed philanthropy and omniscience for the Bolsheviks whereas critics of the USSR suggested that there was only malevolence and doctrinaire ignorance. But in other ways there was much agreement.

Several writers in the last three decades have proposed a somewhat different way to examine the October Revolution. Their guiding tenet is that the revolutionary transformation was not monopolised by the political elites but also involved the masses acting in their own interest and through their own organisations. Soviets and other organisations came to reject the Provisional Government's policies as well as its right to govern, and the age-old popular contempt for the middle classes encouraged the lower strata of society to run their local communities without heed of the official authorities. The masses had not taken leave of their senses. War, economic dislocation and administrative breakdown meant that their everyday needs were not being met. The sole alternative was for people to take their affairs into their own hands; and as the situation worsened, so the workers, soldiers, sailors and peasants moved towards direct political action. The Bolshevik party had the slogans that most nearly corresponded to their wishes. So the Leninist seizure of power was an easy task: the masses had already completed most of the job for the Bolsheviks.

This school of thought has been described variously as 'history from below', 'social history' and 'revisionist history'; it has frequently been counterposed to the traditional accounts highlighting 'political history' [12]. This is a false polarity. The year 1917 is best analysed by combining the two types of analysis. Thus events at the summit of Russian politics shaped what happened on the lower slopes of society; but the same society developed ideas and forms of activity independently of politicians and parties. It was a process of dynamic interaction.

Politics counted. Lenin used his chances whereas the leader of the Provisional Government, Alexander Kerenski, missed his. Bolshevik ideology had some kind of appeal to 'the masses', and the Bolshevik party conducted a zealous campaign in pursuit of power and revolution. What also needs to be recognised is that the congruence between Bolshevik policies and mass aspirations was never tight and was always likely to be temporary. Lenin manipulated popular opinion by keeping silent about those of his intentions that might lose him popular support [249: *224–8*]. Even this oversimplifies things. Lenin genuinely expected a less arduous establishment of socialist power than was achieved. If he fooled the masses (and fool them he did), he also fooled himself. In order to understand this disjunction, moreover, it is important to note that the political and social transformation between February and October 1917 was not a uniform process. Instead it was chaotic and multifaceted. Across the former Russian Empire there was not one but thousands of revolutions – revolutions in regions, provinces, cities, townships, suburbs and villages. The interests of each revolution were pursued by its activists, and eventually there was bound to be a settling of accounts among all of them. At a time when Russia was being ripped apart by war and her citizens were turning to drastic measures, a peaceful outcome was improbable.

[i]   War and the gathering economic crisis

Much that happened in 1917 derived from the astuteness and audacity of the Bolshevik leaders and from the utopianism which sustained them and which they encouraged among working people. But the revolutionary explosion cannot be understood solely in these terms. Economic and military conditions afford a useful starting point for analysis. As the fighting continued into 1915, the Russian army adapted quite adequately to the gruelling novelty of trench warfare [273: *68*]. But the railways became overloaded and under-maintained at a time when priority was given to transporting conscripts, munitions and food to the Eastern front. The rail network, barely able to cope with all its freight traffic in peacetime, had trouble in getting sufficient grain from the south to the grain-deficient provinces of central and northern Russia in the war's first full year [262: *7–8*]. Urban rationing was seriously contemplated. Good harvests in 1914 and 1915 were followed by a drop in cereal production in 1916 by 10 per cent below the annual average for the half-decade before the First World War [296: *3–5*]. It is true that more wheat remained in the Russian Empire because of the German naval blockade, but the peasantry marketed much less of it than previously [160: *70*]. Some peasants were ruined by the wartime chaos, others held out for higher prices or else fed more grain to their cattle and turned more into illicit commercial vodka [272: *374*].

There was neither the time nor the money to restore the railways; and the higher prices necessary to tempt the peasantry to sell its grain were unaffordable by a government that was committing most of its resources to the army on the Eastern front and to the armaments factories. Metallurgy and mining were crucial to the army's operational capacity, and they secured favourable treatment from the Imperial government. Instant solutions did not exist. The government, after raising emergency loans from the Allies, coped by printing huge quantities of paper currency. This resulted in inflation. The peasantry felt even smaller incentive to put its harvest on to the market. A. A. Rittikh, Minister of Agriculture, threatened in November 1916 to introduce a state levy of grain at fixed prices, but the measure was not enforced for fear of antagonising the peasantry.

The industrial situation added to the problems. Production of agricultural implements crashed to 15 per cent of the pre-war level [303: *10*]. There was little a peasant could buy even if he had a mind to. By 1916, nearly four-fifths of the machine-construction business was being assigned to the requirements of the Imperial forces [160: *325*]. Industry by and large satisfied the state's demands in this respect. Hundreds of factories were converted to military work, but the unavoidable consequence was that output for the civilian market steeply declined. Governmental contracts for shells, rifles and greatcoats had the attraction of a guaranteed profit. But not all enterprises obtained such contracts; and any firm that was not engaged in war-connected activity had difficulty in getting hold of raw materials. The dominant mining cartel Prodamet, based in Ukraine, caused havoc for small and medium-sized firms by not selling them enough iron. The impaired condition of the railways worsened things and as early as 1915 there was the start of a fuel and metal shortage. Talk by 1916 was of crisis: it was already foreseeable that the armaments-manufacturing sector would soon be thrown into disorder.

The incompetence of the Imperial administration was not the chief cause of this. A couple of years of war were bound to accentuate the defects of an economy not yet as modernised as that of the German enemy. Disruption would have occurred in the economy whichever other political group – whether liberal or socialist – had been in charge of the war effort. Production and commerce would be severely dislocated so long as the state needed to keep millions of conscripts well equipped and adequately fed. No change was likely while Russia remained at war.

[ii]   Social commotion

Such a situation boded ill for the Imperial monarchy. The country's entry into the war induced a brief political lull; and even many revolutionary activists shared in the general desire to defeat the Central Powers. But there was no end to the growing economic disorder, and workers and garrison soldiers were going hungry. The increasing size of the labour force in factories and mines made for an additional difficulty. By the end of 1916 there were nearly 3.5 million such labourers, and the conscription of a quarter of working men into the armed forces meant that the influx into industrial employment was even more remarkable than it seemed [122: 72, 75]. The pressure on housing stock was relentless. A bad situation was worsened by the flood of refugees from the German-occupied territories who had to be accommodated. Shelter also had to be found for peasants who were recruited for work in the factories. Conditions deteriorated as streets and sewers failed to be repaired [124: 20–1]. The squalid tenements of St Petersburg, which was renamed Petrograd to give it a non-Germanic resonance, were notorious. Elsewhere, especially in the mining towns, the standard of daily life for workers was even direr. Discontent mounted after the brief burst of patriotic support for the government at the start of the war.

It is true that real wages rose somewhat in the metalworking factories [165: *86–7*; 193: *89*]. But employers were intensifying work routines and failing to maintain safety standards. And skilled metalworkers, however much they earned, could only buy what groceries reached the shop shelves. Food retail turnover sharply decreased. Bread queues lengthened. The result was that workers returned to seeking the regime's removal. Waves of strikes pounded official Russia in late 1915 and again in late 1916.

The British and German governments, too, were hit by labour unrest, but not with the same intensity. Nor did they have to navigate such storms of disaffection among the middle classes; not even the badly listing hulk of the Habsburg monarchy was yet being battered to this degree. In Russia the doctors, lawyers, teachers and members of other 'free professions' found the state's bureaucratic structures still more irksome than before the war. Newspapers reported on the filthy, ill-equipped hospitals on the Eastern front. Rasputin's closeness to Empress Alexandra offended everyone. A sexual liaison between them was rumoured. The atmosphere thickened as stories spread that 'dark forces' were at work against the country's interests. Alexandra, a German by birth, was said to be exerting influence in favour of peace with Germany or worse – perhaps she wanted to open up Russia's military defences to the Germans. People of all classes blamed any wartime difficulty on treason, whether it happened at the front or in the rear [120: *259*].

The government and high command exacerbated the social mood by its own policies. It expropriated German businesses and deported Germans, Crimean Tartars and other 'suspect' national groups from the Russian and Ukrainian hinterland; it also refused permission for Jews to move out of the Pale of Settlement even though they were under threat of occupation by the Central Powers. Some national and religious groups were implicitly categorised as more dependable than others [182: *127*, *137–57*]. Ministers were at first reluctant to conscript Moslems for fear of offending religious sensitivities about how the Imperial armed forces were organised. But the shortage of military manpower forced the government's hand, and the predictable consequence was an outbreak of disturbances in regions where Islam was strong. Orders were also given for the formation of new military units based on the ethnic principle [244: *75–6*]. But the emphasis was on relying predominantly upon the empire's Slavic subjects. This caused annoyance to the others. Just as dangerously it inadvertently seemed to give sanction to Russians in Moscow and elsewhere to join riots against any German nationals and even simply persons or businesses with German-sounding names [182: *31*].

The authorities were diffident about restoring order since they badly needed to sustain a patriotic spirit. Nor could it afford to appear gentle on the German minority. The dilemma was a sign of the slender thread which bound government and people together. Popular impatience with the regime was growing and the police were wholly inadequate at keeping it contained.

Even many industrial employers turned against the government. Those with the profitable war contracts, whose base of operations was the factories of Petrograd, were pretty content. But elsewhere the disgruntlement was strong. In Moscow, many firms were either too small or too orientated towards producing civilian consumer goods to gain a share in the wartime financial cake, and the opposition to the monarchy became entrenched among them [107: *30*]. The thin cats wanted to be fat cats. Nicholas II, moreover, could no longer count on much support even from the landed nobility: its young men were perishing as army officers on the Eastern front and their replacements in the trenches tended to be non-nobles who felt less loyalty to the monarchy. Morale among the owners of landed estates meanwhile plummeted as economic conditions deteriorated. The conscription of 14 million able-bodied young men reduced the number of mouths needing to be fed by the average peasant household. This in turn lightened the financial pressure on peasants to work on the gentry-owned estates or to cough up land rents to landlords [157: *6*]. By 1916, even leaders of the Council of the United Nobility were discussing whether a change of regime might be desirable [210: *125–6*]. The branches of the Okhrana were warning by the winter of 1916–1917 that a revolution was imminent. As was usual, the cabinet ignored these unwelcome reports [175: *364–5*].

The emperor and his series of premiers had never treated the Duma more contemptuously. Prorogation, and the threat of it, was the government's wartime sport; and Marxist deputies to the Fourth Duma who obstructed the vote on war credits were arrested. Although police penetration of the clandestine revolutionary parties remained deep, political opposition survived. Negotiations among liberal and conservative groups inside the Duma in 1915 at last produced an agreement to form a 'Progressive Block' of Kadets, Octobrists and Progressivists. This facilitated the joint articulation of discontent among the middle classes. Humiliated in the Duma, these politicians redoubled their efforts in the zemstvos and various voluntary public bodies. The objective was to fill the gaps in the government's coverage of war services. Front hospitals were set up. Also influential were the War-Industry Committees. These were private institutions, established both at factory level and nationally, that had the regime's grudging permission to improve co-ordination in production and supply. Their existence was construed as proof of the authorities' administrative bankruptcy.

[iii]   The February Revolution of 1917

Yet the thoughts of the Progressive Block about a coup against Nicholas II did not yet reach far beyond the stage of talk [187: *124–7*]; the soundings taken by Octobrist leader Alexander Guchkov in December 1916 were the sole serious exception. Liberals and conservatives still worried that a revolution might lead to an eruption of the fury of the 'masses'. The workers' organisations were the monarchy's most dangerous adversaries. Not a few industrialists thought it impolitic to go on allowing the factory workforces to send representatives to the War-Industry Committees, and undoubtedly the legal sickness-insurance funds were being used by revolutionaries to encourage political unrest [199: *372–3*]. The government vigorously suppressed strikes in late 1916; it also quelled a revolt in central Asia by Moslems unwilling to be conscripted into the Imperial Army. Its nerve seemed unbreakable. But the reality was different. Workers remained implacably hostile to the regime and trouble broke out in February 1917 when women textile workers went on strike in the capital. They were quickly joined by the men from the nearby armaments works. Petrograd was in turmoil as demonstrations against the authorities filled the central thoroughfares. The metropolitan garrison mutinied rather than obey orders to suppress the disturbances. Nicholas II's decision to dispatch an armed expedition from the Eastern front was made too late. In any case, the disenchantment had spread even to the high command hundreds of miles to the west at Mogilëv near the Eastern front. All loyalty to the emperor had vanished.

The February events were complex. The workers had rebelled and the soldiers had refused to fire on them. The strikes, demonstrations and mutiny could still have been quashed if the coercive agencies had kept faith with Nicholas II. There was no certitude that the last knell of Romanov power had tolled. What made the difference, ultimately, was that the middle-ranking enforcers of order on the streets had lost their will to use violence to maintain the status quo. The revolutionary party activists shrugged off the worries afflicting them since the *Okhrana* had smashed their little groups in December 1916; and behind the scenes the elites of Duma and big business were gleeful. The Allies quietly also approved. But it was the workers and soldiers and not the politicians, administrators, generals, businessmen and ambassadors who acted. A revolution requires action, audacious action. Action came in the form of strikes, demonstrations and mutiny in central Petrograd.

On 2 March, the bewildered Nicholas II consented to abdicate. The ultimate pressure had been applied by a group of Duma politicians, who proceeded to form the Provisional Government. It was adherents of the Progressive Block who predominated in the cabinet, and Kadets were its majority. Georgi Lvov was chosen as premier. Ministers swiftly promulgated civic freedoms of speech, assembly and association and promised to hold rapid elections, with a universal adult franchise, to a Constituent Assembly. They aimed to keep Russia in the war. Initially they disguised their objective to fight on for all-out victory and territorial gain. They refused to decree an agrarian reform because they wanted to hold over the land question for resolution by the Constituent Assembly. A concern for procedural niceties was evident here. The Kadets were also reasoning pragmatically that if they decreed a transfer of land to the peasantry, the result would be the disorganisation of agriculture and defence since peasant conscripts would desert to their villages to acquire their share of the local landowner's estate [240: *127–8*]. The attempt was applied with equal eagerness to the workers' organisations. Kadets urged them to be

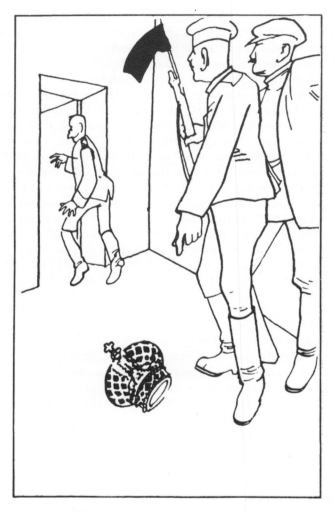

Cartoon 3   D. Moor's cartoon from 1917. Revolutionary soldier addresses Nicholas II:

'Citizen, take your crown along with you.'

moderate in their wage demands. The Provisional Government stressed that military security would be threatened if industrial disputes dragged on. Such judgements required an abstention from social radicalism. In 1905 the Kadets had drawn up a plan for the compulsory dispossession of the nobility's landed property, albeit with financial compensation. For some years they had been less keen to highlight schemes of this sort; they saw that if they hoped to attain governmental authority, they needed to throw in their lot with Russia's propertied elites. The events of February 1917 aggravated their trepidation about workers and peasants. To say the least, there was a lack of enthusiasm in their arrangements to put their governmental mandate to the test of Constituent Assembly elections.

The physiognomy of the Kadets as the catch-all party for the protection of urban and rural middle-class interests was no accident. Even industrialists who had profited from close links with the old regime welcomed the Provisional Government; and few among the reactionary diehards of the gentry actively opposed the Kadet-led administration.

Yet the writing was already on the wall. In setting up their cabinet, the Kadets and their partners had to maintain amicable relations with a mass organisation thrown up in the course of the February Revolution. This was the Petrograd Soviet. The capital's workers and soldiers had elected it to protect their interests. The Provisional Government owed its very existence to the Soviet's acquiescence and 'dual power' was built into the post-revolutionary settlement. The uneasy symbiosis of Government and Soviet in the capital had its parallels across the country as workers, soldiers and even some peasants established soviets and other sectional mass organisations. If anything, the fragility of the governmental apparatus was greater in the provinces. The cabinet dismissed the old governors and appointed its own commissars, who were to work in consort with the various 'committees of public safety' that sprang up after the monarchy's overthrow and which were usually led by liberals [299: *11–13*]. Such bodies did not last long. The cabinet extended the authority of the municipal councils and the zemstvos. But these had to be elected on an unrestricted franchise for the first time and the voters were quick to show disapproval of the Kadets. Problems were great for the Provisional Government in Russia and greater still in the non-Russian regions. The official reluctance to grant more than limited autonomy to local representative institutions aroused hostility in Ukraine and Finland. Throughout the country, moreover, state power was paltry. Not even the Russian Orthodox Church was friendly to the Kadets. Its clerics, freed from centuries of governmental tutelage, fell into strife among themselves about how to organise ecclesiastical authority and about what new rituals were approvable [256: *258–62*]. Meanwhile the police had been disbanded in the February upheaval, and the garrison soldiers were treated warily by the Lvov cabinet.

The gap between the government and popular opinion was as yet a crack rather than a chasm. The workers with their street demonstrations and fighting had brought down Nicholas the Bloody, and yet they stood aside as a 'bourgeois' cabinet assumed power. Some Bolsheviks wanted to set up at least the temporary socialist government that they had intended since 1905. Their frustration grew and they attracted people who felt likewise [245: *78*]. But the working class in general did not think in such terms. Not yet.

[iv]   Aspirations in society

Workers at this stage recognised their numerical weakness in relation to the rest of the country and believed in the need for political unity among the various social classes. The last thing they wanted was a civil war [189: *82*]. Their aspirations were still in the condition of development but probably, as before the Great War, they desired a democratic republic, an eight-hour working day and higher wages [113: *154*]. They rejected the objective of territorial expansion in the war; in their view, the armed forces' job was simply to defend the frontiers [165: *241*]. The workers were already proving their determination in the first days of the February Revolution. Dignified treatment at work was demanded. Polite forms of address became obligatory: everyone was to be known as citizen, including the former emperor [114: *303–4*; 268: *23*]. Obnoxious managers and foremen were daubed with red paint or tossed in a sack before being carted around the factory in a wheelbarrow; some of them were thrown into nearby rivers. Such actions were designed to indicate that the humiliation of working people would no longer be tolerated [263: *55–7*]. Wage rises were demanded. Employers did not immediately give way since their traditional preference for confrontation over cautious concession had not wilted. But the workers held firm, and the settlements reached in spring led to increases in real wages and to more consultative methods of handling disputes.

Civil servants and members of the professions gave less trouble. Support for the Kadets was strong among them; and the Provisional Government, after sacking the old provincial governors and officials in the Ministry of Internal Affairs, left the state bureaucracy intact and experts warmed to the greater appreciation of their expertise. Personnel in other agencies though were more hostile. Although most army and navy officers accepted the new cabinet, the troops were less easily satisfied. Killings of martinets occurred in February [193: *14*]. The Petrograd garrison prodded the Soviet into issuing Order No. 1 whereby they would no longer salute off-duty officers or be addressed in insulting language. Above all, soldiers elected their own committees to protect their interests. The Provisional Government yielded, and the reforms were extended to the rest of the armed forces. Troops in the garrisons were politically more aggressive than were those at the front, but all conscripts welcomed the concessions and swore allegiance to the cabinet. Yet they also increasingly declared that their loyalty depended upon the authorities convoking a Constituent Assembly, restricting military operations to defence and seeking to negotiate a continental peace [300: *287, 321*].

Such a development which was unparalleled in the armies of the other combatant countries greatly restricted the cabinet's scope of action. Ministers continued to talk confidently. They were pleased that the countryside had been tranquil in the February Revolution. Soldiers, who were drawn predominantly from the peasantry, showed greater restlessness than their families back in the villages. But this contrast was of a temporary kind. The Provisional Government's postponement of land reform annoyed the rural millions. For centuries peasants had said that the land should belong to those who worked on it. Most of them in Russia wished the commune to direct such a transfer and half-measures were not going to placate them. Negotiations with landlords were usually friendly and peaceful in March 1917, but violence also occurred. In the ethnically Russian provinces 183 disturbances were reported in the same month [170: *88*] and 49 cases of arson were registered [200: *848*]. The peasantry was acting in historical character. Customarily it had put up with its lot for decades and then suddenly, when an external crisis affected the villages, it had risen up in pursuit of its particular demands. The lack of political sophistication among peasants in no way diminished its capacity to menace the post-autocratic order. The peasantry wanted the land, and at last had a perfect opportunity to take it.

[v] 'Dual power'

Ministers looked round for an agency capable of restraining politi-cal radicalism. They thought they found what was needed in the soviet leadership. The Mensheviks and the Socialist-Revolutionaries headed the soviets by virtue of having won the earliest elections to them. These two socialist parties accepted the Provisional Govern-ment on condition that it would protect the civic freedoms and fight only a defensive war against the German and Habsburg empires. Their long-term aims were for the complete transformation of soci-ety; their socialism was of a radical nature. They became known as moderate socialists mainly because they did not seek power for themselves at this time. The Kadets, for their part, were hoping that the Mensheviks and Socialist-Revolutionaries would dissuade work-ers, peasants and soldiers from demanding too much from a cabinet which had inherited a host of acute wartime problems.

This compromise initially gave some grounds for optimism. The Mensheviks, who had totalled a handful of thousands before February 1917, quickly became a mass party after the February Revolution and by autumn had about 200,000 members [174: *389*]. The Socialist-Revolutionaries recruited in the countryside as well as in the towns, and with a vaunted figure of 1 million members [221: *236*], were easily the largest party. Neither the Mensheviks nor the Socialist-Revolutionaries wanted govern-mental office in the current circumstances. The alliance between them disguised deep programmatic disagreements. The Men-sheviks as conventional Marxists of their time assigned the lead-ing role to the urban working class in the eventual achievement of socialism, and they admired large-scale, centralised forms of organisation in state and society. The Socialist-Revolutionaries, following the traditions of Russian populism, extolled small-scale and decentralised organisational arrangements; they emphasised the positive potentiality of the peasantry. Even so, a substantial convergence of the two viewpoints had occurred over recent years. The Socialist-Revolutionaries' ascendant leaders, unlike the populists of the 1870s but like the contemporary Mensheviks, considered that the Russian industrial economy required further capitalist development, so as to build up the country's productive strength and cultural resources, before socialists tried to assume power [142: *105–8*]. In any case, the Socialist-Revolutionaries aimed at a revolution by and for all 'the toiling people' and not just the peasantry [212: *80–1*]. Both parties judged that wartime was the worst imaginable situation for going it alone and risking economic catastrophe through a break with the bourgeoisie [282: *245, 312*].

Their conditional support for the Provisional Government was a logical consequence. This involved turning a blind eye to the evidence about the expansionist war aims of the Kadets. The harmony was broken in April when Foreign Minister Pavel Milyukov notified London and Paris that the Provisional Government stood by the secret treaties signed by the Allies in 1915 and expected to be rewarded with territory around the Black Sea at the expense of the Ottoman Empire. The Mensheviks and Socialist-Revolutionaries in the Petrograd Soviet feeling betrayal of trust organised a protest demonstration. The Lvov cabinet met in fevered session and, under pressure from the Soviet, Milyukov and Guchkov resigned.

The other ministers concluded that their liaison with Mensheviks and Socialist-Revolutionaries had to be made closer. Lvov invited the Petrograd Soviet to supply representatives for a coalition cabinet. The Soviet's Executive Committee, after some hesitation, complied and from May 1917 the ministerial set-up included a minority of socialists. The most energetic incomers were the Mensheviks Irakli Tsereteli and Matvei Skobelev and the Socialist-Revolutionary Viktor Chernov. They were committed to changing governmental policies at the expense of their Kadet colleagues. Tsereteli worked to arrange a conference of socialist parties from all combatant countries in neutral Sweden with the purpose of pushing all governments into terminating the war. Skobelev introduced measures for the improvement of factory workers' welfare and for the increased state regulation of industry; this provoked the resignation of the Progressivist A. I. Konovalov [240: *269–73*]. Chernov disapproved of the government's refusal to implement agrarian reform and discreetly allowed the transfer of unused agricultural soil to the peasantry through the channels of locally elected land committees [128: *102–3*].

These initiatives by socialist ministers had slight practical effect. The Stockholm Conference never met and Skobelev's measures barely infringed the private interest in the Russian industrial economy. As for the land question, Chernov's fiery statements outside the Provisional Government's chambers in the Tauride Palace were a symptom of his impotence to transform policy within them. The Kadets were not giving up without a struggle. They were helped by the conviction of their socialist colleagues that the proper time had not yet arrived for them to be holding power. Moreover, Mensheviks and Socialist-Revolutionaries continued to believe that the most acute threat to 'the Revolution' came from the political right. The danger of a military coup was never far from their thoughts. This was another stimulus for them to hug close to the Kadets as being lesser demons than an army dictator. Kadet ministers went on arguing their case. They had always demanded a reopening of a Russian offensive on the Eastern front, and in June 1917 persuaded the cabinet to order an attack on the Austrian sector in Galicia. There was initial military success for the Russians. The Austrians called in German reinforcements, and the Russian General Alexei Brusilov's forces ended up digging new trenches in Ukraine to stabilise the front line.

[vi] Economic breakdown and social reactions

Events at the summit of the Russian state were anyway a subplot in the main drama of 1917. Both the working class and the peasantry in army and countryside were actors in their own history. Politicians everywhere talked of clashes between the 'centre' and the 'localities', between 'the top' and 'the bottom', between the 'authorities' and the 'elemental masses'. They thought everything topsy-turvy. Only one large party, the Bolsheviks, welcomed the situation. Workers experienced worsening material conditions and, because they had always felt shunned by the Russia of property and power, they blamed the deterioration exclusively on the middle classes. But employers too were having a hard time. Profit margins in the heavy-manufacturing factories were around 9 per cent [285: *281*]. Although this figure was slightly higher than the pre-war average, it presumably refers solely to those enterprises which stayed operational throughout 1917 and in any case tells us nothing about the light-industrial sector. A truer index of the plight of all manufacturing is the fall-off in monthly coal output by 27 per cent between January and August 1917 [285: *289*]. Factories across the country as early as April were receiving less than two-fifths of the metal supplies needed for the fulfilment of contracts [285: *185*]. Inflation accelerated; transport difficulties increased. Closures of enterprises began. As food supplies to the towns declined a state monopoly in the trade of grain was proclaimed in March. There were also measures to introduce urban bread rationing, but the norms could not be held to and cuts were made successively in April and June [144: *96*; 285: *457*]. The wage settlements, furthermore, failed to keep up with the rise in prices [165: *132*].

The callousness of employers towards their workers was no myth, and the textile millionaire P. P. Ryabushinski was not alone in praying that 'the bony hand of hunger' would compel workforces to soften their demands. But industry would have been likely to collapse even if owners and workers had got on better. A shortage of capital and raw materials had been growing before the February Revolution and industrial disputes merely worsened an already worsening situation. The urban working class dreaded a possible winter of starvation. Although strikes still took place, their effectiveness was fading at a time when employers were cutting back on production. Workers urgently needed to maintain their jobs in a working factory. Meanwhile the noisy mass meetings inside the gates of the enterprise convinced many industrialists that labour productivity would continue to fall. Workers, on their side, resolved never to be done down again. They stuck together, skilled and unskilled, male and female, old employees and new. They understood that a common threat existed to their livelihood [263: *198–9*], and they were united by the belief that a fairer world than that of capitalism could be constructed. Factory committees, elected by workers, were empowered to supplant existing managers if closure seemed imminent. 'Workers' control' became a rallying cry in Petrograd from midsummer.

The origins of this movement were self-protective. The industrial labour force wanted to defend themselves against losing employment and being thrown on to the streets to starve. Previously the workers had often been divided by skills, trade and district [119: *469*]; now they showed solidarity. It was essential for them to prevent the lockouts being announced by employers. There was an upsurge in popular talk about the 'dark forces' ranged against working people [114: *154–7*]. Whether the workers could truly have halted industry's descent into the abyss is doubtful. The basic problems were fundamental, and certainly could not have been solved in wartime. Nevertheless the workers had to do something. The alternative was total despair.

The disaffection of soldiers, especially in the garrisons, exhibited a similar motivation. The June 1917 offensive demonstrated the Kadets' determination to win the war, and ever more troops were alarmed by the thought of being used as cannon fodder. Desertions were not yet a massive problem in July and August. But distrust of the Provisional Government was spreading. The fact that the daily availability of food was unreliable instigated further discontent. The attitude of soldiers and sailors was disturbing in itself. It also provoked worries in the cabinet that no military force remained to deter the peasants from doing whatever they liked. The official procurement agencies in the eight months of the Provisional Government's existence obtained only 48 per cent of the country's grain requirements [285: *442–3*]. The government frantically doubled its fixed agricultural prices in August, but no lasting improvement resulted [285: *431, 442*]. The peasantry's opposition was no longer merely passive. When the government continued to declare that the Constituent Assembly alone should decide the agrarian question it was spitting into the wind, illegal land seizures became frequent. Meadows were an early peasant objective; three-fifths of occupations of pastures took place in June and July. Arable land was grabbed at a steady rate from May through to October. Mere residence by landowners was treated as resistance. Killings occurred. Violence in general was plentiful; at the peak of the trouble, in July, 481 'disturbances' were reported [128: *204*].

[vii]   Mass organisations

In most provinces of European Russia it was the land communes that co-ordinated such activity just as factory committees did in the towns. The Bolsheviks had almost no impact on this. Few villages saw any of the party's agitators. The cities and towns were where the Bolshevik party committees were based. Bolsheviks were suffering from a general shortage of experienced manpower. Consequently opponents of the party who attributed the spread of revolutionary sentiments predominantly to Bolshevik influence were overstating the case. Workers and peasants – and perhaps also the urban lower middle class – took up radical political ideas without much prodding from the Bolsheviks. Equally exaggerated was the charge that all would have been fine if only 'the intelligentsia' had not led 'the masses' by the nose. That is not to say that intellectuals were without importance. In the local soviets their skills were at a premium [19: *116*]; and at the national level, in Petrograd, they were very prominent. But the intelligentsia was a divided stratum. Some intellectuals, such as Vladimir Lenin and Lev Trotsky, were fiery Bolsheviks; others, such as Tsereteli, belonged to socialist parties which tried to restrain the working class from direct action on the streets. In addition, the leading soviet politicians included ex-workers such as Menshevik Kuzma Gvozdev. The incidence of middle-class leaders anyway was probably slight in the factory committees [263: *190–1*]. Possibly it was not much greater in local trade union branches. The various mass organisations showed that working people could mobilise themselves with vigour in defence of their interests.

The monarchy's overthrow had allowed the entire society, including the nobility, to join in the democratic enthusiasm. Every social group, big or small, set about electing its representatives. Debating and demanding became a regular activity. Governmental power remained frail and steadily the soviets turned into a potential alternative government. In June they held their first national congress, which chose an All-Russia Central Executive Committee led by Mensheviks and Socialist-Revolutionaries to conduct business across the country. Commissions were created to keep watch on the ministries of the Provisional Government. These were hectic times and the Central Executive Committee, with its dozens of members, was too unwieldy to respond rapidly to sudden changes in circumstance. Authority was devolved to an inner Presidium and, eventually, to a core of prominent officials such as Tsereteli who were dubbed the 'Star Chamber'. Kadet ministers were alarmed by the assertiveness of the central soviet machine as well as by their own ineffectualness in imposing governmental decrees on the country. They disliked the trends in policy, especially when the Mensheviks and Socialist-Revolutionaries insisted on granting regional autonomy to Ukraine. In the eyes of Kadets, this was a first big step to the territorial dismemberment of the state, and they collectively resigned from the cabinet in the first week of July.

Intensive consultations followed and Kerenski, a Socialist-Revolutionary veteran and a minister since the February Revolution, became premier. Kerenski put together a new coalition cabinet. This time there was a majority for the moderate socialists from the soviets and only four Kadet ministers. On the face of it, the Mensheviks and the Socialist-Revolutionaries had taken power by stealth. The reality was different. Kerenski's policies contrasted little with those of the Kadets except in rhetoric. His record has attracted much casual disdain. The moderate socialists were in fact not endeavouring to accomplish something outlandish. Their aim was to prevent economic collapse by unifying political groups on the right and left. Suffice it to add that nothing had occurred since the February Revolution to jolt most Mensheviks and Socialist-Revolutionaries into thinking Russia ready for socialism. If anything, events seemed to validate their scepticism. Economic ruin and military setbacks continued. There were increasing signs of social disorder; Chernov himself was nearly lynched by workers and sailors in Petrograd in July. A final struggle to achieve a reconciliation of all classes appeared appropriate.

The central soviet leaders, while looking as if they had installed a socialist administration, shuddered at the very notion. They studiously avoided giving unnecessary offence to the Kadets; and the result was that an alternative government, if it was to be established, had to be initiated from another source. This occurred in the provinces. Slowly in summer 1917, like blank photographic paper revealing its image in a developing bath, a political revolution was manifesting itself. Not all town soviets across the country were as diffident as the Central Executive Committee in the capital; those in Kronstadt and Tsaritsyn, being bitterly opposed to the Provisional Government, were with difficulty dissuaded from declaring themselves independent republics [126: *96–7*; 225: *207*]. Others were less hostile to Kerenski but tended nonetheless to supplant the official bureaucracy in several normal governmental functions. They set up militias to police their area. They provided food kitchens and educational facilities; they campaigned against hooliganism [268: *25*]. To celebrate their revolutionary achievements they held festivals. Their word could countermand orders by garrison commanders; they could intervene directly in the workings of their local economy. Such developments were not confined to Russia. Outlying cities, like Baku on the Caspian, evolved similarly [274: *119, 131*]. Menshevik and Socialist-Revolutionary leaderships in the town soviets distant from the capital had willy-nilly been drawn into encroaching upon the prerogatives of the local agencies of the Provisional Government. Where they held back, the suburb soviets often pushed in and did the job instead. The common trend was for lower soviet bodies to ignore their hierarchical superiors whenever conflicts over policy arose [288: *235*].

This explains why workers, soldiers and peasants kept faith with 'the soviets' and with the idea of 'soviet power' even while the Central Executive Committee was refusing to accede to their demands for more radical reforms in the economy and society. Mass participation in the discussions in the soviets continued through 1917. The open meetings supplied a forum for the voicing of popular opinion, and plenary sessions of soviet deputies were seldom held in camera. Deputies could be individually recalled for failing to represent the constituency's wishes. Admittedly, the system was prone to abuse: executive committee sessions became less well attended; general elections of soviets were held at longer intervals; functionaries acquired imperious ways of dealing with their constituents [19: *124–6*]. By and large, though, local soviet bodies were responsive to requests from below. They recognised that this was the prerequisite of their authority in such a tumultuous environment. The clearest warning to them came from the workers. In spring 1917, many soviets tried to temper working-class aspirations; the factory labour force countered by playing institutional leap-frog and jumping across to other mass organisations such as the factory committees to achieve their wishes [263: *179–81*].

[viii]   The Bolshevik party

The fluidity of such politics was bewildering. It placed a requirement upon all parties to react swiftly, sensitively and decisively.
Only the Bolsheviks achieved this. Their success was intimately
connected with the fact that they were the only big party uncondi-
tionally hostile to the Provisional Government. Their standpoint
was clear by April. They wanted the government to be over-
thrown and replaced by an administrative structure based upon
the soviets. They wavered a little, dropping the slogan 'All Power
to the Soviets' in late summer when their prospects of enhancing
their position in the soviets seemed poor. But the abandonment
was temporary. On the war, moreover, Bolshevik policy was constant. They aimed at an immediate general peace. They argued
that a socialist revolution in Russia would spark off revolutions in
Germany and elsewhere, and that these would put an end to the
fighting without annexations or indemnities. They also called con-
tinuously for national self-determination in the former Russian
Empire and throughout the world. Their economic objectives at
home included governmental ownership of the large industrial
firms and all the banks. Land nationalisation was another objective, which was expected to take the form chiefly of the peasantry,
seizing non-peasant fields and cultivating them for private profit.
The Bolsheviks would hold the Constituent Assembly elections.
They confidently predicted a victory that would justify the taking
of power by the soviets (which, as sectional institutions, denied
representation to the middle and upper social classes). This pro-
jected dictatorship involved a modification of strategy. Until 1917,
Bolsheviks had expected autocracy's demise to be followed by a
lengthy epoch of rule by bourgeoisie. Now they wanted to com-
mence the transition to socialism without delay. The party leader
Vladimir Lenin expressed these fresh ideas in his *April Theses*.
On his return from Switzerland, he noted that many Bolsheviks
had by themselves come to the same conclusion. The April Party
Conference witnessed a triumph of the new line [245: *46, 53–4*].

The Bolshevik party was loosely structured. Its formal rules
demanded that rank-and-file members, activists, officials and
lower party bodies should obey higher bodies. But its Central
Committee could not automatically secure compliance. Persuasion
counted for a great deal. Equally decisive was the agreement of

nearly all Bolsheviks about the key immediate goals. This consensus was in embryo in March. Opposition was at its strongest in the Central Committee but was quickly surmounted; at lower levels, those party members who objected left the Bolsheviks [245: *49*]. The process had its difficulties. Thousands of rank-and-filers remained hostile to the division of the Bolsheviks and Mensheviks into separate parties; but by midsummer, such inhibitions had evaporated because of disgust with Menshevik collaboration with the Kadets. The road was open for the consolidation of an anti-war, pro-revolution mass party; and the Bolsheviks grasped the opportunity. A few thousand people considered themselves Bolsheviks in February 1917. By late summer it was being claimed, with some exaggeration, that the figure had soared to a quarter of a million. The influx was not confined to rank-and-filers. Merely 83 per cent of Party Congress delegates in July 1917, according to an official questionnaire, had been Bolsheviks before the First World War; and perhaps as many as 23 per cent had previously adhered to the Mensheviks or other parties [245: *43, 49*].

What made this party so dynamic an agency of revolutionary activity was not its mutterings of dogma. Nor was it just Lenin's tactical acumen. Far from it: his judgement was sometimes badly awry [249: *310–12*]. In mid-June, for example, he encouraged the holding of an armed demonstration of workers and sailors against the Provisional Government; and it was only at the last moment, in the first week of July, that he recognised his impetuosity and tried to call it all off. The postponement came too late. Troops fired on the demonstrators and the arrest of prominent Bolsheviks, including Lenin, was ordered. Lenin escaped to Finland. Luckily for him this personal débâcle did not dissuade an ever-larger number of supporters in the factories and garrisons from favouring direct political action. Workers were said to constitute around three-fifths of the members in late 1917 [245: *43–4*], and this enabled committees in the provinces to stay in touch with popular mood as it developed. Local issues were often as important as those of wider significance in the political campaigning of the Bolshevik party [71: *240–1*]. Not infrequently the so-called 'party masses' pushed their committees towards more radical measures. The attitude was fierce and exalted and, as material conditions worsened, a little desperate too. Highly 'democratic' and highly 'authoritarian' ideas co-existed in Bolshevik thought; and party

Cartoon 4   A. Strakhov's cartoon from 1924, showing a stylised Lenin with factory chimneys in the background. In fact Bolshevik newspapers avoided showing pictures of anyone in 1917, and Lenin shaved off his beard and moustache before the October Revolution.

members at all levels, even in the Central Committee, felt under little obligation to resolve the contradictions of their future policies in advance. There was a belief that 'practice' would fill in the lacunae of 'theory'. This optimism was misplaced, but it did no harm to the party's drive for recruits and electoral backing. The Bolsheviks came to seem attractive by virtue of being the only group truly believing that the horrendous difficulties of war economy and government were immediately surmountable.

[ix]   Disintegration of the state

The polarisation of Russian politics proceeded without cease; and, as the Bolsheviks' popularity in the towns increased, so did their representation in the various mass organisations. First factory committees and then, not long afterwards, soviets came under their influence. Petrograd, Kronstadt and Tsaritsyn were areas of early success. That this was happening by September was a tribute to the party's resilience. The arrest of Trotsky and other leading Bolsheviks in the capital as well as Lenin's flight into hiding in Finland were accompanied by a campaign of vilification in the press. But these were minor setbacks. Bolshevism had always claimed to be the people's bulwark against counter-revolution, and Kerenski found he could not repulse the forces of the far right without their assistance. Kerenski's manoeuvres were of labyrinthine complexity. In order to reassert his authority in Petrograd, in August he ordered Commander-in-Chief Lavr Kornilov to transfer combat troops to the capital. At the last moment he suspected Kornilov of intending a coup d'état. Kornilov, meeting the threat of his own arrest, concluded that a coup was indeed desirable since Kerenski had lost the will to subdue the unruly soviets. Bolshevik as well as the Socialist-Revolutionary and Menshevik activists hastened out to persuade Kornilov's units to disobey their commander. The Petrograd garrison could not have stopped him. But the political mission succeeded and Kornilov was taken into custody. The Bolsheviks then renewed their campaigning without even the harassment from the government that had bothered them since July [218: *158–9*].

Fortune was with them. There was little chance of conscripts wanting to join the national anti-socialist brigades like the Freikorps which marauded German cities from late 1918. The Provisional Government had no such contingents at its disposal. Russian workers and peasants had never been responsive to nationalist slogans. They continued to live unperturbedly along-side the other national and ethnic groups and to recognise that poor material conditions were not peculiar to the Russian nation. Solidarity among 'the working people' in Russia cut across other potential dividing lines for the duration of 1917. By contrast, nationalism was on the rise in the outlying regions of the former Russian Empire; and was a further thorn in the Provisional Government's flesh. Ukraine was becoming ungovernable from Petrograd and its own elected *Rada* held the real power in Kiev. Finns, Armenians, Azeris and Georgians were also seeking greater freedom for themselves [279: *96–7*]. Kerenski was understand-ably getting frantic. He could not even, as a last resort, appeal for direct foreign intervention. The British and French armies were bogged down in the battles in the West. The Americans had joined the Allies in spring 1917 after German attacks on their shipping, but their troops did not arrive in France until 1918. The Provisional Government was on its own.

The Provisional Government experienced only harm from its linkage with the Allies. The offensive on the Eastern front in late June had been a disaster with Russian military frailty displayed for the world to see, the British and French cabinets completed the humiliation by excluding Kerenski's diplomats from discus-sions on the post-war territorial arrangement to be imposed on the Balkans. The government's helplessness was still more cruelly exposed when, in August, the German army smashed through the defences on the Baltic littoral and took Riga. Any further advance would have jeopardised Petrograd too. Kerenski, politi-cally weakened, had to hearken more attentively to the desires of his Menshevik and Socialist-Revolutionary contacts. The Kadets were cool towards him in August when he summoned a 'State Conference' in Moscow to assist all parties and public organisa-tions from the far right through to the far left in getting together to deliberate on the country's travail; they resigned again from the government on the eve of Kornilov's putsch [240: *229*]. Kerenski then convoked a Democratic Conference in September. This event was arranged on a narrower basis; not only the far right but also the liberals, who had scandalised socialist opinion by condoning Kornilov, were discouraged from participating. The Conference agreed on the need for the kind of policies pushed by Tsereteli and Chernov in the first coalition cabinet and for the formation of a cabinet without the Kadets. But tamer thoughts prevailed. Kerenski wanted Kadets in his team, and some proved willing to join it [240: *244–6*].

[x]   The October Revolution of 1917

The Bolsheviks treated the Democratic Conference with contempt, attending only long enough to declare the need for a socialist programme, and then left. The danger of moving too fast was recognised by their Central Committee. They sensibly cast aside Lenin's counsel to seize power without further ado. They went on building up their base in the soviet infrastructure while Kerenski's authority shrank daily. The expectation of a Bolshevik seizure of power grew. The blithe hope was nurtured, by groups from the Kadets across to the monarchists, that Lenin's party would quickly be crippled by the onus of office.

Not all Bolsheviks were convinced that a favourable moment had arrived. Lenin lunged back into the reckoning. He had a limitless capacity to persuade and goad. On 10 October, the Central Committee debated the question of state power. Lenin returned clandestinely from Finland to participate and the consequent decision came from his pen. Still he had to be restrained. He wanted to seize power immediately. Trotsky successfully recommended the Central Committee to time the uprising so as to enable state authority to be grasped on the opening day of the Second All-Russia Congress of Soviets. Thus 'soviet power' would be established and the appearance of a coup by a single party could be avoided. Even so, there was uncertainty about the strength of active support for the Bolsheviks in Petrograd. Even many leftists in the party reported on workers' lack of enthusiasm for violent measures. But adequate forces were available. The Petrograd Soviet, through its Military-Revolutionary Committee, controlled the garrison; and workers in the Red Guard had the necessary weapons and commitment. These easily overwhelmed the government's guard at the Winter Palace. Popular uprisings have never been organised by a people as a whole. Only a minority directly participates. And, by mid-October, Lenin could reasonably argue at least that soviets in cities throughout Russia were queuing to follow the example of Petrograd and

Moscow in acquiring Bolshevik majorities. The Second Soviet Congress would predictably put the party in charge of the central soviet apparatus. Working-class opinion had swung in favour of Kerenski's removal and it seemed as if the trend was irreversible.

The February Revolution was in the final stages of decay, and some kind of socialist government would very likely have emerged from the chaos in any event. The Bolsheviks accelerated the process. They were willing to adjust policies to take account of demands from the factories: the adoption of the slogan of 'workers' control' in May 1917 was a vivid example [263: *155*]. The bid for peasant support was raised too. Lenin, recognising rural suspicions of his proposal to nationalise the land, declared instead that the land should become the property of 'the entire people'. It was also Lenin's initiative that ensured that the revolutionary government was to take the specific form it did. His leadership combined straightforward statements of intent with careful political fudges to keep the party with him and the working class on the party's side [249: *236–41*]. The transfer of power in Petrograd was not attended by lengthy conflict. The Petrograd Soviet's Military-Revolutionary Committee, directed by Trotski, acted efficiently. On 25 October 1917 the Provisional Government was disbanded and authority was assumed by the Second All-Russia Congress of Soviets.

3 Experimental Construction, 1917–1927

What explains the Bolshevik party's survival in power? Textbooks in the USSR gave a confident answer to this question. Their argument was that the party had not and could not have anticipated every emergency; but they claimed that its fundamental principles saw it through and that the Soviet government's social and economic reforms made it permanently attractive to most workers, peasants and conscripts [27; 28]. Foreign observers, at least those outside the world's communist parties, went along with this. Detractors asserted that really the Leninist regime was unpopular and that only dictatorship kept Lenin and the Bolsheviks in power. The Bolshevik party was supported only by a minority in society. It conducted a savage terror to win the Civil War and maintain itself in the peace that followed. It had a fanatical leader in Lenin as well as fanatical doctrines. Reinforcing the worst traditions of tsarism, it imposed an appalling one-party regime and exploited the cultural backwardness of the society it ruled [30].

This left plenty of room for disagreement on other matters. Some writers suggested that when Lenin seized power, he genuinely wanted to found a 'democratic' state and that he was pushed into dictatorship by unanticipated difficulties and by political and military resistance. Others retorted that he and his party had always been in favour of a terror regime, but had kept quiet about this until they were in government. A further bone of contention has been the periodisation of early Soviet history. Lenin's fiercest antagonists argued that the regime was constantly repugnant. Others saw the New Economy Policy, which was introduced in 1921, as a respite from the early excesses [7; 21].

All this was linked to the question of the internal imperatives of the one-party state. One answer was that the Bolsheviks had to remain uncompromising and aggressive in order to survive. But such a notion was contested. Some commentators suggested that once the Civil War had been won, the door was open for the phasing out of political dictatorship and social intimidation and for the construction of a truly democratic socialism. The whole topic continues to be controversial in later writings on the early Soviet one-party state. Common to these writings, whether they were for or against the Bolsheviks, was the assumption that the outcome of the October 1917 Revolution was explicable mainly in terms of the actions of political leaders. Attention has recently also been paid to social and economic factors – and indeed to politics below the central level. Such an analysis stresses that the Soviet government and communist party had a substantial degree of support across the country [12]. A few, indeed, argue that the Leninist regime was truly not very dictatorial at all. But others restrict themselves to asserting that the dictatorial outcome was nowhere near as preordained as the older writers contended.

Among the themes of the newer writing is the impact of culture upon politics. Russians, it is suggested, had never acquired ideas of tolerance. The First World War and Civil War brutal-ised already brutal feelings and practices [4]. But if this was so, it was not just a matter of culture. There was also an administra-tive factor. The Bolsheviks, if they wanted to impose order on the country, had to rule firmly. Transport and communications were chaotic. Sabotage was frequent. The potential for rebellion by the regime's political, religious and national enemies had not disappeared, and economic conditions were dreadful until the mid-1920s. The wish to regularise the situation by establishing a one-party state and to introduce centralist, disciplinary methods was shared by Bolsheviks and their supporters. Lenin did not impose centralism against his party's wishes: its officials in gen-eral recognised its desirability. So the contours of dictatorship and terror were shaped to some extent by pragmatic reactions to a difficult situation [246]. No doubt, too, the isolation of the Soviet regime in Europe and Asia reinforced the existing Bolshevik need to reinforce the tight and authoritarian characteristics of the one-party state.

The wheel of interest had been turned away from the importance of individual leaders, of political decisions and of ideology to the outcome of the October Revolution. The events of the first decade of Soviet power are shown to have complex social, economic, administrative and international underpinning.

The argument in this chapter avoids adopting one approach to the exclusion of all others. Lenin's way of consolidating power was inherently dictatorial. His party's doctrines were highly authoritarian even before 1917 and no Bolshevik felt discomfort in engaging in civil war and acute 'class struggle'. Without this leadership and ideology there would have been no Soviet state of the kind that actually arose. The party was not the slave of circumstance. For example, it took the initiative in approving the Brest-Litovsk Treaty with the Central Powers in March 1918 and bringing in the New Economic Policy three years later. It also arranged the institutions of the Soviet state according to its wishes. It set up a quasi-federal constitutional structure which allowed non-Russians to have their own republics within the USSR. But the Bolsheviks were constricted by the antagonisms they encountered. They were handling political and social ingredients that were not infinitely plastic. The entire situation in which the party found itself gave rise to problems: a shattered economy, an intolerant political culture, an administration accustomed to arbitrary methods, a crudification of attitudes by the years of war and revolution and national, social and religious antagonisms which had been held in check by tsarism but which had been drastically heightened since 1917.

Such a mixture would probably have been a devil's brew even if the Bolsheviks had not been stirring the pot. If they themselves had not been so utopian, so ruthless and so fixated on staying in power, there might have been a prospect of some attenuation. But the Bolsheviks were what they were. They did not achieve the revolutionary transformation they had dreamed of in 1917. This was hardly surprising. Their dreams had been incoherent, implausible and unrefined by any experience of government. In power, they had to experiment to survive. And they typically chose options that first and foremost would make them secure them against counter-revolution. A bad situation was made greatly worse, and from this situation sprang the tragedy of revolutionary Russia.

[i]   Euphoria and aversion

The Bolsheviks had seized power by an armed political coup in the capital knowing they would be supported by most workers, many soldiers and, with a bit of luck, a large section of the peasantry. They expected their action in Petrograd to be followed by popular uprising; and indeed there were insurrections in several Russian towns, and the peasants grabbed the land once the change of government had taken place. Meanwhile, on Bolshevik instructions, the Military-Revolutionary Committee of the Petrograd Soviet arrested opponents and closed Kadet and right-wing Menshevik newspapers in their first week in government. Although they lacked a detailed, long-term plan, the Bolsheviks had a set of basic guiding assumptions – and these assumptions were quickly stripped of any residual indulgence to their opponents.

The Second Congress of Soviets, controlled by Bolsheviks, installed a Bolshevik government. Its name, as abbreviated in Russian, was Sovnarkom; the fuller version was the Council of People's Commissars. The 'chairman' was Lenin, who wrote a Decree on Peace calling for an end to the war on the basis of national self-determination. The independence promised by the Provisional Government to German-occupied Poland was confirmed; and Finland was granted hers. The party hoped this would encourage a socialist revolution in both those countries and everywhere else [249: *285*]. The 'European socialist revolution' was predicted as imminent. Meanwhile in Russia the Bolsheviks nationalised many of the largest factories and all the banks. Foreign trade was brought under governmental supervision and Sovnarkom unilaterally annulled the debts left by the administrations of Nicholas II and Kerenski. 'Workers' control' was introduced in industry so that the labourers of each enterprise might keep a check on their managers. Bolsheviks expected a quick reversal of industrial decline and restoration of trade of commodities between town and countryside. They also sought an alliance of the proletariat and the peasants, especially the poorer ones. A Decree on Land was issued. It authorised peasant soviets to oversee the redistribution of the estates of crown, church and nobility and to expropriate non-peasant land without compensation.

On 25 October 1917, 'soviet power' extended little beyond Petrograd. But Kerenski's attempt at a counter-coup with mounted Cossacks was a charade and the City Soviet acted through its Military-Revolutionary Committee to secure the capital for the new administration [235: *51–2*]. The Bolshevik-led soviets in other towns followed suit, adapting their tactics to the specific local challenge they faced [151: *153, 279*]. In northern and central Russia this was a rapid process. Fighting lasted several days in Moscow. In Ivanovo-Voznesensk the worst commotion occurred with an uproarious singing of the 'Internationale' to celebrate Sovnarkom's creation. In some Volga cities, in Russia's south-east, conflicts were bloody. But generally the strife was of short duration and low intensity [19: *362–70*].

Urban Russia was under rule by soviets by the beginning of 1918. Yet the mainly non-Russian inhabitants of cities in Ukraine and the south Caucasus still sought autonomy from Petrograd's control; and soviets on the periphery of the former Russian Empire declaring allegiance to Sovnarkom, as in Baku in Azerbaijan, were rarities [269: *226–7*]. Closer to home, in Russia, the peasantry refrained from offering direct support for Lenin's government. For a while the Bolshevik party remained buoyant. Problems existed only to be solved, or so it seemed at the time. Bolsheviks were funnelled into posts in the soviets and other state agencies. Institutions proliferated. The party leadership not only took over surviving organs of government but also, since these often proved inadequate to their tasks, set up several new ones. There was broad scope for local initiative, and the transfer of authority to the soviets in Saratov induced the hyperbolic announcement: 'Our commune is the beginning of the worldwide commune. We, as the leaders, assume full responsibility and fear nothing' [202: *57*]. Bolshevik party leaders in Petrograd assented. Y. M. Sverdlov, the party's central organiser, contended that the government's decrees provided only general guidance and that it was up to the localities to get on with their own revolution [241: *61*]. 'Mass practical work' was Lenin's refrain. The release of the people's creative potential was as great a priority for Sovnarkom as direction from on high.

[ii]   Economic and military prostration: 1917–1918

This orientation was possible only so long as the party continued to underestimate Russia's economic and military emergency. The sceptics in the Central Committee, such as L. B. Kamenev and G. E. Zinoviev, had little following. Lenin issued ultra-optimistic predictions for some weeks – and this was the general standpoint of Bolsheviks at the time. Meanwhile a catastrophe impended.

There were already plenty of signs of it. In 1917, the large and medium-sized factories had produced only two-thirds of the output registered for the year before the First World War. Production in such enterprises in 1918 tumbled to a mere third of the previous year's record. The industrial economy was battered to its knees by the transport breakdown, by the inadequacy of supplies of raw materials, by the capital investment shortage and by unchecked inflation. In the first ten months after the October Revolution 38 per cent of the country's large factories had to close [130: *34*]. The agrarian sector fared only a little better. The harvest of summer 1917 was down only by 13 per cent on the annual average for 1909–1913. But here too the beginnings of trouble were discernible. The country as a whole was left with a deficit of 13.3 million tons of grain to meet what had been regarded as normal standards of consumption. Even southern Russia and Ukraine lacked a surplus to 'export' to other regions, and the Volga area reported a shortfall below its internal needs [290: *7, 15–16*]. The situation was aggravated by the fact that ruination of manufacturing made it hard to acquire even half-satisfactory food supplies for the towns because there were too few industrial goods to send to the countryside in exchange.

The Bolsheviks, like the Provisional Government before them, attracted all the blame. But there were positive aspects in Sovnarkom's measures: nationalisation and workers' control kept many operated which would otherwise have been liquidated by their owners, and profiteering rackets ceased. The authorities also tried hard to deliver such manufactured products as did exist to the countryside. Yet the adverse effects of policy weighed more heavily. The party's ultimate goal was the extirpation of capitalism, and this destroyed all confidence among businessmen. Lenin himself did not intend the instant, comprehensive introduction of socialism; but he was not the entire party. His colleagues spoke menacingly about entrepreneurship. Even the Bolshevik eagerness to end the war made for problems. When the government ceased to finance armaments production, the war-orientated factories – which constituted the majority – were unable to switch

to civilian work overnight. Disruption was the predictable result
[101: *36, 38*].

The Soviet republic's foreign relations were also in trouble.
Trotsky, as People's Commissar of External Affairs, quipped that
his task would be to publish the ex-tsar's secret treaties and retire
to await the inevitable global conflagration. But the fuse smoul-
dered damply in the winter of 1917–1918. Riots, strikes and mutinies in central and western Europe did not lead to revolution,
and German diplomats demanded that Sovnarkom should cede
sovereignty over the west of the former Russian Empire. Trotsky's
trick of dragging out the negotiations conjured up a few weeks
of non-conflict. But in January 1918 the Germans delivered an
ultimatum. For most Bolsheviks, both at the centre and in the
localities, this left no option but to wage a 'revolutionary war'.
Lenin judged differently, arguing that the refusal to sign a separate peace with Germany and Austria-Hungary was the politics
of the kindergarten. In February, as German military superior-
ity became manifest, others in the party reached the same conclusion. Nikolai Bukharin and other so-called Left Communists
found support waning for military action. The Seventh Party
Congress in March 1918 sanctioned the signature of 'the obscene
peace'. By the terms of the Treaty of Brest-Litovsk the Soviet government abjured its claims to Ukraine, Belorussia and the Baltic
region. This involved the loss of two-fifths of the country's industrial resources. It dashed hopes of economic reconstruction and
political stabilisation through the emergence of friendly nearby
states. It hugely worsened the food-supplies difficulty. The loss
of Ukraine meant that grain would have to be procured from
regions which could not even feed their own inhabitants [290:
14–16].

[iii]   Social reforms and mass participation

Yet the Bolsheviks survived. The elite in every social revolution
needs to hold on to the favour of broad layers of the population.
In 1917–1918, Sovnarkom's social reforms enjoyed much support among workers, peasants and soldiers. The ethos of popular
self-liberation and participation remained in evidence. The party
did not yet direct all public affairs; on the contrary, many changes

at the base of the economy and society were made independently of governmental decrees. Working men and women in late 1917 were reportedly 60 per cent of the Bolshevik party membership and their presence ensured for the moment that the aspirations of 'the masses' were taken seriously.

Factory workers in some places went beyond Lenin's idea of 'workers' control' as a means whereby the work force could supervise managerial personnel. Instead they entirely ejected their old owners, managers and foremen [258: *228*]. This initiative was warmly received by the left wing of the Bolshevik party, which changed its name to the Russian Communist Party in March 1918. The leftists were equally pleased by demands from below for a more far-reaching policy of nationalisation. Lenin by contrast had wanted to take only the 'commanding heights' of industry into state ownership; he also exempted medium-sized and small factories from governmental takeover. Several work forces simply 'nationalised' their firms without consulting Sovnarkom [100: *99*]. Such actions reflected a zeal to create a new society, free from oppression and exploitation. There was also a desperate bid to impede factory shutdowns [241: *232–4*]. Utopianism and pragmatic concerns were entwined. Local economic agencies welcomed working-class functionaries in the hope of curtailing the influence of officials inherited from Nicholas II and the Provisional Government [129: *282–5*]. Bolshevik theory extolled the urban proletariat as the vanguard of socialist revolution. Many workers in any case required little prompting to engage in public affairs; they had brought down the Romanov monarchy and wanted to go on having an impact upon the political process.

The auguries for disappointment were already present. The general economic situation led to massive unemployment. The average number of gainfully employed factory workers in 1917 fell by 23 per cent in the following year [227: *9*]. Unskilled labourers were the worst affected; factory committees exhorted them to return to their villages, if they could, to fill their stomachs. The privilege of staying in the towns, even with a job, was no sinecure. Starvation had become a realistic fear. In Petrograd, in February, it was necessary to reduce the official bread ration to a few ounces per day.

Workers understandably began to put the interests of their particular enterprise before state interests. Disruptive localism was denounced by the government in town and countryside. Nearly 50,000 'agitators' had sped out to the villages by midsummer 1918 to explain central policy [87: *4*]. But peasants wanted and got their own revolution. Both the October 1917 Decree on Land and the Basic Law, which was enacted four months later, sanctioned this. The clauses that annoyed the peasantry, like the ban on breaking up the large capitalist estates, were ignored in the villages [19: *395, 400–1*]. The communes strengthened their authority. Although regional differences persisted, a pattern was widely clear: by 1920 only 4 per cent of peasant households in 39 provinces of European Russia existed outside the communal structure [66: *209*]. The peasantry continued to confiscate land. In Russia's central agricultural region, peasants gained direct control over an area about a quarter larger than had previously been in their ownership; and in Ukraine it was around three-quarters [66: *181–2*]. Yet few became instantly rich. Nearly all families gained so little land that even a Ukrainian-style increase would not save them from poverty: land-hunger persisted. Most of the fields seized by the peasantry in 1917–1918 had anyway been rented and farmed by peasants for years. So the actual area under their cultivation expanded only slightly. Yet the advantages accruing as a result of the Revolution were not trivial. A little land was better than no extra land at all. Payments to landlords ceased and mortgage debts were annulled; and peasants enjoyed looking out upon a landscape from which, it seemed, an oppressive state administration had been permanently removed.

They showed no gratitude for this. Annoyed by the rising inflation and the dearth of industrial products on sale, they kept their grain to themselves. The state meanwhile remained responsible for feeding the towns and the armed forces. It could have persuaded peasants to bring their harvest to market again by revoking the ban on free trade in grain, but the People's Commissariat of Food Supplies argued that this would necessitate a further cutback in rations. Outside the capital there was growing alarm and several local soviets temporarily suspended the grain monopoly [208: *56*]. People elsewhere survived by illegal bartering. Sovnarkom would have been more prudent to requisition a bare minimum of supplies and to allow the peasantry to sell the remainder privately. This solution was becoming more practical in the winter of 1917–1918 as many soldiers and workers left for their native villages and ceased to depend on being fed by governmental agencies. An ideological factor made the suggestion unfeasible. The Bolsheviks found it repugnant to show greater indulgence to private enterprise than Kerenski's government had done. The alternative was to use force. Authorities from some towns adopted this option in early 1918, and impounding of grain followed. Clashes with the peasantry occurred [19: *431*].

[iv] Repression

All this was a blow to the Bolshevik premise that the working class and peasantry should stay in alliance. But if the party leadership was a victim of circumstances, it was a victimiser to a still greater extent. Bolsheviks had always regarded peasants as less reliable than workers. Some leaders were annoyed that a scheme to make peasants stop farming for profit had not been imposed; they argued for socialist agricultural collectives to be set up [287: *95–6*]. Their cries were ignored for a while but the party's impatience with rural intransigence mounted.

Bolshevik political intolerance was not confined to the countryside. Lenin and Trotsky opposed proposals for Mensheviks and Socialist-Revolutionaries to join Sovnarkom because of their participation in the Provisional Government. Several Bolshevik Central Committee members and People's Commissars were aghast at this. It is an index of the patchiness of the party leadership's thinking that an insurrection had been carried through without prior discussion about who was to belong to the new government. When Lenin and Trotsky now got their way, their dissenting colleagues resigned; and the rupture of negotiations with the Mensheviks and Socialist-Revolutionaries affronted those countless workers who had backed the seizure of power on the assumption that a regime uniting all socialist parties would be formed [162: *226, 335*]. Mensheviks and Socialist-Revolutionaries anyway were refusing to join a government that included Lenin and Trotsky; they hoped that the other Bolsheviks would bring their party to its senses. Perhaps a socialist coalition could then be formed. Not everyone preferred peaceful methods. The forces of the political right were reappearing when General Mikhail Alexeev gathered a Volunteer Army in southern Russia. Not a few Kadets wished him well; some were even to prove willing to welcome German occupation if it would facilitate the overthrow of Bolshevik rule.

Lenin and Trotsky in fact were not absolutely averse to coalition: they asked the Left Socialist-Revolutionaries, who were breaking away from the Party of Socialist-Revolutionaries, to join Sovnarkom in the early days of the October Revolution. The invitation was initially rejected. But eventually, in November, the Left Socialist-Revolutionaries became the junior partners in the Soviet government.

The Bolsheviks had in any case done more than anyone else to initiate the cycle of intolerance. Before seizing power, Lenin had mitigated his vocabulary of civil war and dictatorship whenever he thought workers might take fright [249: *226*]. But he intended repression; he ordered arrests and newspaper closures in his very first week as Soviet premier whereas the rival socialist parties were reluctant to risk armed conflict. The creation of an Extraordinary Commission (or *Cheka*) in December involved the crossing of a fateful threshold. The purpose was to eradicate counter-revolution and sabotage without the requirement to follow judicial procedures in collecting evidence and carrying out sentence. Then, on 5 January 1918, came the first session of the Constituent Assembly. The Bolsheviks had done well in the towns, especially among the working class. But their party received only 21 per cent of all votes. The Socialist-Revolutionaries, with their huge rural support, did massively better with 38 per cent and this did not even include the backing for their sister parties in non-Russian regions [222: *30*]. It was the first freely contested election in the country's history – and the last for over seven decades. Sovnarkom flatly refused to abide by the result. The Constituent Assembly was forcibly dispersed; scores of persons were shot in street demonstrations. The urban working class, moreover, had never been monolithically pro-Bolshevik. The economic conditions and the spectacle of violence strengthened the dissent. In spring 1918, the Bolsheviks were defeated in several elections to city soviets in central Russia. Again the polls were ruled invalid. In Petrograd, where Bolshevik authorities kept a tighter grip upon the City Soviet, thousands of hostile workers went ahead and formed an Assembly of Plenipotentiaries. Force was used to crush it [80: *181*].

The government survived not just because its coercive agencies were fierce but also because popular approval of Sovnarkom's early economic decrees remained widespread. The promotion of factory labourers into public office, in addition, strengthened the Soviet state internally; and the party itself could still boast that most of its rank-and-file members were of working-class origin. The chances of overthrowing the Bolsheviks were weaker than they seemed. Hunger, unemployment and the flight from the towns cut back the potential for organised resistance. Although the soviets had been bases for independent social activity in 1917, they required many more years of favourable circumstances if they were to maintain their integrity against the Bolshevik resolve to bend them to the party's will. Disunity and low morale among the anti-Bolsheviks made Lenin's task easier.

[v]   Civil War: 1917–1921

It was in this dire situation that civil war broke out. All seizures of power striking at the roots of property laws are likely to involve violent struggle. In China in 1949 and Cuba in 1959 the old regime's demolition was the culmination of the fighting. In Russia, the October Revolution signalled the first approaches to protracted warfare.

Soviet forces were sent into Ukraine in December 1917 and took Kiev. Their success was short-lived. To the north, the German military menace compelled the capital to be transferred from Petrograd to Moscow in February 1918, and the Brest-Litovsk treaty necessitated the Soviet withdrawal from Ukraine. In May, a further contraction of territory occurred. A legion of Czech former prisoners-of-war rose in revolt against Sovnarkom. They swept aside the Bolshevik-led soviets from Siberia through to the river Volga. For months, Nicholas II and his family had been held in detention in the Urals. The Soviet authorities were afraid that the Czech legion might liberate them, and had all the Romanovs executed. The retreat before the Czechs continued. Reaching Samara, the Czechs lent support to a government of Socialist-Revolutionary members of the Constituent Assembly; and yet another administration, representing several anti-Bolshevik parties, was set up in Omsk in Siberia. Meanwhile the

Left Socialist-Revolutionaries, infuriated by Brest-Litovsk and by grain requisitioning, walked out of the Sovnarkom coalition and organised a brief revolt against the Bolsheviks in Moscow.

The woes of the Soviet state went on increasing. The Volunteer Army, now commanded by General Anton Denikin upon the death of Generals Alexeev and Kornilov, was on the move in the Russian south. In the autumn, Admiral Alexander Kolchak assembled a contingent of reactionary Imperial officers in Siberia. These two White armies, as they were called to distinguish them from the 'Reds', had little intention of restoring the Constituent Assembly. In fact the first action of Kolchak's followers in November was to crush the Omsk government backed by the Socialist-Revolutionaries.

Sovnarkom had been organising a Workers' and Peasants' Red Army since February; it rushed its troops under Trotsky's fierce, dynamic leadership down to retake the Volga cities in late summer 1918. This descent into all-out war strengthened the moves made by Bolsheviks to overhaul the institutions of the Soviet state. Centralism, discipline and demarcation had begun to be introduced in a piecemeal fashion in early 1918, when the organisational disorderliness was recognised as hampering governmental effectiveness. Political disputes too had been causing disruption. The controversy over Brest-Litovsk had nearly broken the Bolshevik party asunder. From midsummer 1918, with the drastic worsening of the situation at the front line, the case for hierarchical authority became irrefutable. The party was transformed. The Bolsheviks, long-time theorists of organisational centralism, were at last practising what they had preached; and power at the party's apex was devolved from the Central Committee to two inner subcommittees in January 1919. The Politburo was to decide high policy and grand strategy, the Orgburo to oversee internal party administration. Power was accrued to fewer officials in local party bodies. The party's functions, moreover, were expanded; in effect it became the supreme agency of state. In 1918 there had been confusion between the duties of Sovnarkom and the Central Committee. The Politburo's rise to ascendancy was a process of lasting importance [246: 86–7].

The new arrangements were not quite as neat in reality as on paper. The party lost personnel to the Red Army armed forces, which meant that its supervisory capacity was limited at times

[75: *197–8*]. Both the army and the Cheka retained much independence in their day-to-day operations. But results, not formal means, were the Politburo's priority. Its own internal procedures were flexible. Lenin on occasion issued instructions after a telephone conversation with his Politburo colleagues, but without a proper meeting. The waging of war, in the belief of Bolsheviks, necessitated exceptional measures. Violations of Soviet legislation were condoned so long as they aided the military effort. The style of work throughout the state was frenetic. It was also intimidating. Trotsky, as People's Commissar for Military Affairs, employed thousands of officers from the Imperial armed forces to staff his Red Army. To each of them he attached a 'political commissar' to ensure loyalty, and he also took hostages from their families. Yet he also promoted individuals whose careers had been baulked before 1917. Just as workers were becoming civilian administrators, so NCOs were rising to ranks of command.

The party strengthened its appeal to nearly all the non-Russians. The notable exceptions were the Cossacks. Among the Bolsheviks their name was a byword for counter-revolution, and a blatant attempt was made at ethnic cleansing in 1919. Thousands perished in the process of de-Cossackisation before it was halted for pragmatic reasons [141: *178*].

Bolsheviks otherwise strove to reach out to diverse peoples. Their early hopes had proved exaggerated. When given their independence in December 1917, the Finns neither established a socialist government nor applied for membership of the Soviet state. Bolsheviks altered their approach, and national self-determination ceased to be offered. The Red Army was charged with the task of reconquering the lands of the former Russian Empire; its leadership was not asked to hold plebiscites about state frontiers. Once brought under Soviet control, though, many people were offered the assurance that their national, religious and cultural aspirations would be respected. Ukraine, Belorussia, Estonia and Latvia acquired their own Soviet republics that, at least formally, had equal status to the Russian Soviet Federal Socialist Republic (RSFSR). Inside the RSFSR, the Politburo ordered the establishment of autonomous national republics. Scope was given for schooling and for newspapers in the local language and encouragement was also given to people of every nation to join the party and help the Soviet regime spread its influence. The Bolsheviks wanted to avoid the charge of being imperialists with red insignia. International revolution, indeed, remained the objective. Links were sought with far-left political groups abroad; and in March 1919 the founding Congress of the Communist International (or Comintern), which was to unify and direct communist parties around the globe, was held in Russia.

'Everything for the front' had become the slogan. Campaigning against the White armies of Kolchak and Denikin began again in spring 1919. By autumn, both were defeated. Kolchak's forces had retreated deep into Siberia in midsummer. Their plight left the Red Army free to roll back Denikin's two-pronged attack along the Volga and across Ukraine. In October a third White army under General Nikolai Yudenich moved out from Estonia on to Petrograd in October. Although Yudenich came close to taking the city, a successful defence was mustered by Trotsky and he was defeated. Kolchak was caught and executed in February 1920. Denikin handed over his command to General Pavel Wrangel, but this last White army's breakout from the Crimean peninsula was short-lived. In autumn 1920 the Civil War's outcome was put beyond doubt when Wrangel's forces were evacuated across the Black Sea.

Victory for the Red Army, according to Soviet spokesmen, was achieved to a large extent through the government's alteration of economic policies. The changes had begun in early 1918 and were strengthened as the fighting intensified. Lenin's objections to immediate nationalisation of all industrial enterprises lapsed. Nearly all large factories were state-owned by January 1919, and virtually all medium-sized ones by the end of the same year. The spurt of confiscations made valuable stocks available for the war effort [130: *46*]. Universal labour obligations were introduced and the urban propertied classes were compelled to toil as snow-clearers and defence-works diggers. Strict discipline was demanded in factories. Goods produced in the cities were to be dispatched mainly to the Red Army [130: *38*]. Food distribution was given the same priority; and forcible requisitioning of grain, which had been practised spasmodically in early 1918, was turned into a comprehensive system. Collaboration was sought from the less well off peasants. In May 1918 the government instructed each village to establish a 'committee of the rural poor'. This would enable the authorities to identify the richer families hoarding a food surplus. In February 1919, a further step was taken when the People's Commissariat of Food Supplies designated a total delivery quota for each province. Armed urban detachments were created to impound the subtotals assigned to particular districts and communes. It was a grim process: grain was seized even where peasants needed all of it to feed themselves and have enough left for sowing [92: *170–1*; 147: *178*].

Such measures were a practical reaction to a worsening situation. There was also an ideological element at work. Bolshevik ideas, fired in the kiln of the party's powerlessness and persecution before 1917, retained their robustness. The party held on tightly to its desire for a deprivatised, moneyless, centrally controlled economy. Even Lenin, who before seizing power had proposed a more cautious pace of change in industry and agriculture than many leading Bolsheviks liked, was caught up in the excitement. The economics of this 'War Communism' were not very successful by most standards. Factories in 1920 produced a mere seventh of the output in 1913; and governmental procurement of grain in 1919 fell to a third of the total even for 1917 [130: *34*]. Meanwhile Kolchak and Denikin received military supplies from Britain and France; and they first assembled their forces in regions rich in grain.

But otherwise the Reds were more fortunate. The triumph of the Western Allies in the First World War in November 1918 brought the German military occupation in eastern Europe to an end. What is more, the British and French contingents which disembarked in Archangel and Odessa respectively saw little action and the Allies anyway suspended their intervention at the end of 1919 – the Bolsheviks had consistently, albeit understandably, overestimated the threat they constituted [150: *80*]. Kolchak and Denikin made trouble for themselves by talking about their vision of 'Russia one and indivisible'. This caused offence and fear among non-Russians. In particular, the anti-semitic mayhem of White officers had the effect of securing the Jewish population on the Bolshevik side [259: *168*]. Latvians too supplied highly effective units to the Reds. Even Cossacks, whom the Bolsheviks had initially subjected to repression, were willing to form a Red Cavalry. The use of horses in the roadless countryside was important. The mode of fighting was highly mobile and the cross-trench techniques of the First World War became redundant. The Whites were constantly hampered by the geography of the railways. The Bolsheviks, never losing Moscow and Petrograd, kept hold of the two centres of communication and transport and the regions where the majority of potential conscripts lived [24: 274]. Neither side had a monopoly of strategical error. But the Red Army's chances of recuperation were greater, and there was no White leader with the imaginativeness of Lenin, Trotsky, Sverdlov or Stalin.

It is doubtful that most people, whenever they were free to choose, endorsed either the Reds or the Whites [183]. But the Reds succeeded in gaining a greater amount of active civilian support than any White army obtained. Kolchak and Denikin themselves did not advocate the seizure of gentry land back from the peasantry, but their subordinates were uncompromising reactionaries. Peasant 'ringleaders' were hanged; landed estates went back to the old landowners in areas under White occupation. In the towns Bolshevik party activists and trade union leaders were summarily executed. Compelled to choose between the Reds and Whites, even many Socialist-Revolutionaries joined the Red Army. Kadets filled many posts in the White civil administration but they too met with suspicion from the military commanders [260: 248] – and few Kadets had the nerve to criticise the Whites for their outrages against civilians. The Bolshevik party's programme put it in good stead by comparison. The word went forth in *Pravda*, by 'agit-trains' and on the lips of soldiers and activists: a Red military victory in the Civil War was the sole guarantee that the former ruling and propertied groups would not resume their power.

[vi]   Resistance to Bolshevism

Nevertheless the margin of advantage enjoyed by the Bolsheviks could have been much wider. The Civil War had been a close-run thing and the Reds would have shortened the odds against themselves by abandoning or softening unpopular policies. The Cheka ran amok in the Red Terror officially announced after an attempt on Lenin's life in August 1918. Atrocities were committed against the urban middle class as a whole and especially against former officers of the Imperial armed forces; and several thousand workers and peasants also ended up in prison, sometimes for no more heinous offence than trading in grain in order to remain alive [177: *178*; 230: *280*]. Agrarian measures discredited the party further. The committees of the village poor, set up in mid-1918, were abolished before the year was out because most peasant households resented them. Even so, pressure on the peasants was maintained. In Ukraine, efforts were even made to force them into collective farms [281: *95–6*]. Although the Politburo overruled such schemes, it persisted with grain requisitioning and by 1920 was treating it as a permanent policy. This was inviting trouble. In the same year, party bodies pushed their luck in the towns as well. Factory discipline was taken to the length of transferring military conscripts to 'labour armies' instead of demobilising them. Nor had the ambition to spread the revolution abroad been buried. When the Polish army under Pilsudski seized Kiev in spring 1920, the Reds counter-attacked. A rapid campaign brought them within sight of Warsaw. The Politburo had a 'European socialist revolution' in its sights: Poland was the first target, Germany the second.

Violent upheavals were not unique to the Russian Empire after the First World War. In January 1919, the German Spartacists briefly sustained an uprising in Berlin. In March 1919, Soviet republics were proclaimed in Bavaria and Hungary. The scale and duration of carnage was greatest of all in Russia, and only the fighting in Hungary rivalled it in brutality. Lenin flew into a rage if ever he suspected that the Red Army was failing to kill kulaks and priests; and Trotsky and Stalin were his favourite leading partners in using terror against the urban middle class [251: *65*]. The sufferings were enormous. The country's population declined absolutely by 7 million from 1918 to 1923, with deaths from disease outnumbering deaths in battle [184: *30–1*]. The combatant forces and their leaderships, both civil and military, bore a heavy responsibility for the dimensions of bloodshed, but they themselves were also deeply affected by their involvement in the process. Bolshevism in particular registered the impact. The contest between mass persuasion and massive coercion, in the party's ideas, moved ever more decisively in favour of violence. Harsh abstractions about dictatorship and civil war had lain in the tissue of Bolshevik thought for years. The military strife after the October Revolution force-fed their gross development.

While an army-style authority over society increased after 1918, obedience was a vast distance from perfection as indeed is usually the case with even straightforwardly military governments. The regulation of the industrial labour market proved impossible, largely because of the acute shortage of skilled workers [130: *87*]. Industry survived better in the countryside as artisans left the towns and sold their handicrafts to peasants [115: *286*]. Agricultural acreages, however, went on falling. The area sown to grain in 1921 was down at least 16 per cent, and probably down a lot further still [215: *240*]. Half the urban diet was supplied on the black market by 'sack-men' who bought up wheat illegally in the countryside and sold it in the cities [295: *599*]. Ill-discipline affected even the Red Army. Deserters, including many who simply ignored their call-up, reached a million in 1919; this was not far short of the total of those who actually served at the battlefronts [163: *396, 463*]. Resistance to the Soviet authorities took increasingly active forms. Strikes occurred in Moscow and Petrograd through the Civil War [67; 243: *95*]. Villages were restless. Official spokesmen cautiously admitted that 344 peasant revolts had erupted by mid-1919. In 1920, overt opposition intensified. A rural rebellion gripped Tambov province from end to end [93]. Ukraine and western Siberia too were bases for peasant fighters who were known as 'the Greens' and who hated the Whites and Reds indiscriminately. The strike movement in the cities was in crescendo in the winter of 1920–1921 [224: *93*]. Alarming reports were coming through to Moscow about mutinous talk in the Kronstadt naval garrison.

Peasant insurgents, industrial strikers and sailor mutineers had no chance to co-ordinate with each other but their demands were alike. They called for the abolition of grain confiscations, for a boosting of food supplies, for the reintroduction of free competition among the political parties and for an end to the Bolshevik monopoly of power. The ring of hostile forces tightened. In August 1920, the Polish army unexpectedly vanquished the Reds at the battle of the Vistula and peace negotiations ensued. At home, the Bolshevik party seemed the sole institution on which the Soviet regime could depend. But even this option was problematic. Wartime centralisation had not eliminated friction between local and central Bolshevik bodies. Internal disputes were ferocious. In addition, many workers left the party's ranks in protest against War Communism; less than two-fifths of rank-and-filers claimed to be of working-class origin by 1920 – and even this was probably an exaggeration [241: *148*].

Cartoon 5

"Help!"
D. Moor's 1920 poster of a starving peasant.

[vii]   The NEP and economic recovery: 1921–1927

In February 1921 the Politburo, terrified by the Tambov rural revolt, resolved upon a drastic reform which became known as the New Economic Policy (or NEP). Grain requisitioning was abolished. It was replaced by a graduated tax in kind, and the target set for collection was less than 4 million tons of cereal whereas nearly 7 million had been sought in 1920. Peasants could trade the remainder of their grain legally.

The Tenth Party Congress approved the turnabout of policy in March 1921; at the same time it sent out delegates to put down the Kronstadt mutiny which broke out in the course of its delib-erations. All resistance was to be crushed. No one in the coun-try would be allowed to think that political concessions might be wrung out of the regime. Socialist-Revolutionary leaders were put on show trial in 1922 and sentenced to lengthy terms of impris-onment. The Tenth Congress had already banned factions inside the Bolshevik party. The Democratic Centralists had urged the curtailing of the Politburo's authority; the Workers' Opposition wanted working people to have greater control over economic decisions. Both these factions were suppressed. Lenin argued that internal party unity had to be rigid at a time when a dif-ficult economic retreat was being conducted. Private enterprise returned to industry in 1921. Small factories had traditionally supplied many goods bought by peasants, and, in order to create the conditions to attract rural households into marketing their grain surplus in the towns, the state leased back many such firms to their former owners. By 1923 only 2 per cent of workers in small-scale industry were governmental employees [131: *204*]. Efforts were made to restore commerce with foreign companies. The NEP reintroduced capitalism to Russia.

There were limits to the economic compromises that Lenin was willing to make. Large factories, banking and foreign trade remained in the government's hands. Central industrial planning too remained an objective. During the NEP, the Soviet regime presided over a mixed economy in which the balance of power remained firmly in the hands of the state.

Even so, politics continued to be turbulent. The creation of a one-party state does not by itself completely eliminate strains inside the single party. There were plenty of controversies among

Bolsheviks from 1921. The NEP was a gigantic gamble since no one knew for sure that it would secure sufficient food for the towns. Although the shrinking of the urban population and demobilisation had lowered the government's food-supplies requirements, the tax-collection level set in 1921 was below these lower needs. Families would therefore have to go back to shopping for their food instead of relying on rations [288: *346*; 52]. The riskiness of the NEP became obvious when the 1921 harvest turned out to be a poor one. Hundreds of thousands of peasants starved to death in the Volga region. Diplomatic reverses added to the distress. The French delegation at an international conference in Genoa in 1922 spurned the Soviet request for reacceptance into the world trading community; only the Germans, from among the great powers, would initially co-operate. In addition, domestic pricing policy was mishandled. By 1923 peasants were being asked to pay three times as much for urban manufactured products, in real value, as in 1913. In Trotsky's vivid metaphor, the economy's scissors were opened as the blades of industrial and agricultural prices moved apart. Peasants stopped releasing their grain for trade. The Politburo had to adjust prices in order to close the scissors, and was criticised by Trotsky and other left-wing Bolsheviks for incompetence.

The NEP remained the designated treatment for the ills of the economy. The doses were adjusted to deal with each setback and a general recuperation occurred. This achievement – as well as the coercion used to administer the medicine – helps to explain the policy's widespread acceptance. Agriculture and industry benefited. Grain production in 1926 rose to roughly the same as the annual average between 1909 and 1913. Livestock husbandry surpassed the pre-war years in productivity. The movement to diversify and intensify agriculture, which had begun in the Imperial period, was resumed. In 1913, 90 per cent of the sown area was taken up with cereal cultivation; by 1928, only 82 per cent was needed [298: *4*]. The output of sugar beet, potatoes and cotton increased. Technical advances also took place. There were more horse-drawn machines in annual supply in the second half of the twenties than before the First World War [95: *8*] and multi-field crop rotation was being applied in 17 per cent of sowings in the Russian Socialist Federal Soviet Republic in 1927 as compared with 1.5 per cent for the same area in 1916 [91: *278*]. Such figures give the lie to notions that the agrarian sector slid into stagnancy once it forfeited the benefits of capitalist estate management. In the industrial sector too a lively restoration occurred. Private small-scale manufacturing was resurgent. State-owned factories recorded impressive gains in output. The exact total volume of output in industry remains a contested topic. Some have suggested that by the tax year 1926–1927 it was only slightly lower than in 1913; others propose that it was up to 6 per cent higher [136: *186–7*; 298: 3].

What is beyond dispute is that the NEP involved some successes for the Soviet economy. The decline of investment in industry was reversed [85: *425*]. Engineering capacity outstripped that of the pre-war period, and the proportion of industrial output reinvested in production was no lower than under Nicholas II. The possibility of sustaining an annual growth rate of 6 per cent in manufacturing and mining [298: *270*] was no mean achievement for a socialist state surrounded on all sides by hostile capitalist powers – and 'Socialism In One Country' was Stalin's rallying cry as he sought to convince his comrades that many of the party's objectives were obtainable even in the absence of revolutions abroad. Economic isolation in any case was neither without advantages nor quite complete. The unilateral cancellation of milliards of roubles of governmental debts in 1917 relieved Russia of an enormous financial burden. The UK, moreover, restored trading links with the Soviet republic in March 1921. Trade with the world increased over the 1920s. The export of oil was more than double the volume registered before the First World War [85: *971*]; and the Soviet government, using the revenues in foreign currency as well as attracting concessionaires in industry, strove to renovate the country's technological base. In some key industries, such as oil extraction, the effort met with success [276: *43–4*]. Purchases abroad were crucial. Two-fifths of the machinery and other capital equipment bought in 1926–1927 were imported [85: *413, 971*].

[viii] Social adjustment and survival

Debates on economic strategy were common European politics after the First World War. They were especially intensive and public in Russia. The goal of a mature industrial society was shared by all party and government officials whereas many bureaucrats and landlords had found industrialism abhorrent under the old regime. This aided the economy's recovery. In addition, labour relations were more tranquil than at any time earlier in the century.

At the end of the Civil War, Trotsky had called for the outlawing of strikes. In fact, the working-class gains of the October Revolution were not curtailed so drastically. Industrial stoppages continued to occur. Official reports on the troublesome year of 1927 claimed that only 20, 100 workers were involved; but this was probably a large underestimate [97: *144*; 216: *5*]. The government emphasised the need to remove restrictive work practices so as to raise productivity; time-and-motion specialists toured the larger enterprises – and party-appointed directors enjoyed their privileges like the bosses had always done before the Bolshevik seizure of power [214]. But recommendations for tighter factory discipline were difficult to enforce at a time when discontented workers were consciously hearkening back to the traditions of 1905 and 1917 [242: *40–60*]. And although trade union central leaderships were exclusively Bolshevik and disapproved of strikes in state-owned concerns, their bargaining activity was not wholly perfunctory. The working class, furthermore, gained advantage from the increase in job vacancies under the NEP. In 1920 there had been only 1.2 million labourers employed in the large factories; by 1926–1927 the figure had risen to 2.8 million [85: *955*]. Men who had moved to the villages or served in the Red Army in the Civil War returned to resume their old trades. Women, after being welcomed into the factories in wartime, tended to get pushed out. In 1921, the wages were probably only a third of what they had been in 1913 in real terms [299: *390*], but by the tax year 1927–1928 the tsarist wage level had been reattained and may even have been surpassed by 24 per cent [85: *606*]. For some of the unemployed too there was a degree of improvement inasmuch as the state for the first time in Russia provided financial relief.

While this betterment helps to explain how the regime survived, the forces for social instability persisted. The increase in factory jobs did not eradicate mass unemployment. Indeed over a million workers were registered as unemployed in 1927. Hiring and firing arrangements, even in state factories, could still be peremptory [85: *468–9*]. Small-time traders, known as *nepmany* after the onset of the NEP, strove to make the commercial big time. Shops selling luxury products reopened on Petrograd's Nevski Prospekt; several novels and poems containing indirect criticisms of the Soviet order crept through the mesh of the pre-publication censorship authority, *Glavlit*, which was formally established in June 1922 [76: *79*].

The party's expectation of an uninterrupted procession to socialism had been brusquely shaken. Most workers were hostile or indifferent to the specific boasts of Bolshevism; it galled party propagandists that Charlie Chaplin and Mary Pickford films outstripped those of the Soviet *avant-garde* political cinema in popularity [281: *65*]. The peasantry, in any case, lived unaffected by the mass media, and agronomists and surveyors remained a rare sight in most villages. Under the NEP it was the traditional land communes which regulated the lives of nine-tenths of European Russia's rural households. Atheistic communism made little impact upon the peasantry's Christian faith. Nor did it much affect belief in Islam in the southern and eastern reaches of the USSR [74: *77*]. Sexual habits seem to have altered little in villages or cities [118: *121*]. If anything, behaviour in general became brusquer as the official Soviet authorities subjected the previous standards of social decorum to ridicule [154: *255–7*]. But most people anyway wanted to get on with their lives without interference by the state. A refuge was available in the little informal groups that had existed for centuries: the peasant communes, the workers' *zemlyachestva*, the religious groups and the ethnic and family networks. They had become stronger as the state's intrusiveness increased. Thus the October Revolution and Civil War, while transforming much, had a conservative effect upon society in many ways.

Change was not wholly absent even from the countryside. Younger peasants, gaining confidence from their experiences either in the Revolution or in the Red Army, stood up stoutly to their elders. This was made easier by the growing tendency for sons to leave the family hearth and form their own households. [201: *176*].

Otherwise there was little eagerness to break with most rural customs. In 1917–1918 there had been a levelling of landholding among households and the proportions of the peasantry classified as either rich or poor were reduced. But social differentiation returned with the NEP. Many poor peasants, lacking implements and livestock to till their land, leased it to richer neighbours or worked as their hired labourers. Soviet laws banning this development were unenforceable. The government recognised this by a series of piecemeal measures in the mid-1920s and relaxed several such prohibitions. Social and material inequalities went on growing. By the tax year 1927–1928, 56 per cent of the net sales of grain in European Russia came from merely 11 per cent of households [95: *25–7*]. So were the conditions of the peasantry very different from what had prevailed under Nicholas II? Although the question awaits conclusive investigation, an important piece of the evidence is that more grain stayed with the peasants in the NEP period; the percentage of the harvest leaving the countryside fell from 20 to 15, and quite possibly even lower, to less than 10 per cent, between 1913 and 1926–1927 [85: *941*; 95: *17*]. More peasants, and more of their livestock, ate more and better. Very few 'disturbances' are reported as having occurred in the countryside in the mid-1920s [253].

[ix] The party and the political system

Yet the NEP was no paradise for the peasantry. The real cost of industrial goods in the villages remained higher than before the First World War. The policy involved a balance between the respective demands of many social groups, and those of workers, peasants and administrators were handled with special care by the authorities. Life in the state bureaucracy settled down after the convulsions of 1917–1920, and pay and conditions for civil servants improved. The power of government continued to be imposed firmly. The Politburo's confidence stemmed from the fact that years of repression and warfare had cast down the institutional impediments to its dominance.

The Bolshevik leadership, which had always laid greater store by guiding than by reflecting social opinion, would tolerate no threat to the status quo. State terror was applied intermittently by both army and political police in the mid-1920s [70: *61–71*]. But the scale of such violence diminished after the Civil War. The

Bolsheviks were lords of all they surveyed. Outright counter-revolution had been exported: between 1 and 3 million people had emigrated in the years of turmoil, and these belonged mainly to the middle and upper classes [213: *87*]. Such menace as remained for the Bolsheviks lay not on the political right but on the left. A couple of small, anti-Bolshevik communist parties were formed. But they were easily broken up by the Cheka. The Red Army was trimmed in size. The country was secured against invasion, and internal armed strife, apart from a revolt by the Georgians in 1924 and Moslem guerrilla warfare in central Asia, gave little bother. Still the authorities were leaving nothing to chance. The Solovki island monastery was turned into a prison to hold people arrested for active political resistance. Lenin's Russia in the years of the NEP vastly outmatched Nicholas II's in political unfreedom. The Bolsheviks exercised an unconditional monopoly of power. Before 1917, the most that the monarchy could achieve was to restrict the brood of parties to a scrawny existence.

The Soviet regime was not just a master butcher; it also developed skills at political husbandry. Recognising the suspicions about Bolshevism among adult workers, it sought support among their children. Special efforts were made to appeal to adolescents. Bolsheviks encouraged them to grow up fast and become party militants [153: *77–8*]

Communist leaders also confirmed the new commercial rights even though, it is true, traders and small industrialists still found themselves victims of arbitrary police raids. The climate of business was more stable than since 1917 [73: *39–40*]. Likewise the persecution of the Orthodox Church, after a campaign to traumatise it by arrests and executions in 1922, was slackened. The Politburo recognised that violence against religion would merely provoke unrest; also it particularly wanted to avoid offending those sects whose members were particularly good at farming [186: *183*]. The state exercised its authority in general with greater circumspection and predictability. A high premium was being set upon technical expertise. Non-Bolshevik 'specialists' were attracted into Soviet institutions in growing numbers and Menshevik economists gained public prominence. The favour of non-Russian nationalities too was still courted. In December 1922 the formation of a Union of Soviet Socialist Republics was agreed in principle. While Moscow retained direction over all foreign and most domestic policy, the various territorial units like the Ukrainian Soviet republic nevertheless were given substantial influence over education, health and justice. Talented young non-Russians were encouraged to take posts in the institutions and to further the interests of their respective national group as well as of the October Revolution. Moslems, including imams, in Azerbaijan were recruited to the revolutionary cause [69: *421–35*].

There were limits to Bolshevik adaptiveness. A single party ruled and the Politburo ruled the party. Lenin was not dictator but his persuasiveness and determination usually won the day. Outside the party he retained the chairmanship of Sovnarkom. The complexities of a mixed economy called for detailed decision making beyond the competence of the small central party apparatus. The significance of Sovnarkom increased accordingly [236: *109*]. But when Lenin died in January 1924 the Politburo immediately reinforced its grip. Other central party bodies, notably the Orgburo and the Secretariat, had anyway been growing in authority since the Civil War. A disciplined hierarchy of committees in the provinces was an objective shared by the entire central party leadership, and Moscow's selection and appointment of local personnel acquired a crucial importance. Inevitably the post of General Secretary, held by Stalin from 1922, grew in authority. Shortly before his death, Lenin had decided that Stalin was too crude and unscrupulous, but his bid to eject him from the Secretariat came too late. Under Stalin's control, the central apparatus's regulation of the party intensified. Peremptory commands became typical. Yet the internal party regime was not allowed to petrify into quiet routine. Each local committee secretary had to be hyperactive: he had to show initiative and cut through bureaucratic red tape whenever the Politburo's higher goals were endangered. The NEP's stress upon procedural regularity was far from being absolute. Action and achievement stayed the priority as before [241: *172–3, 207*].

The Politburo did not obtain total satisfaction. The ban on factions in the party could not be fully enforced. Disputes split even the Politburo, and the need for adjudication led to a retrieval of some authority by the Central Committee (and by the Central Control Commission, which was established in 1920 to secure fairness in the conduct of internal party life). Furthermore, Sovnarkom's Commissariats did not accept instructions unquestioningly from the party. Something like pressure group-ings emerged in the political system in the 1920s. As in every coun-try, leaders often supplied advice and information which suited their institution's interests and protected its staff [141: *107*]. Suc-cessive leaders of the Supreme Council of the National Economy, for example, spoke up in favour of boosting state investment in industry [96: *247*]. Inter-institutional alliances based in a par-ticular geographical area flourished informally. Politicians in the Donets Basin and in the Urals had a habit of proposing measures for the rapid expansion of coal-mining [116: *154*]. The Politburo recognised such lobbying for what it was and, by deploying the Workers' and Peasants' Inspectorate to conduct enquiries it tried to avoid being blatantly misinformed. Financial corruption was also investigated [232: *87, 165*]. But the most intractable task by far for the Inspectorate was to ensure that the state's normal, everyday administration was properly handled. Russia remained in many ways 'under-governed, especially in the villages'. The density of the public network of regulation and service was low. Moreover, administrative offices everywhere gained a justified notoriety for insensitivity, and queues of anxious citizens clutch-ing letters of request or complaint were a persistent feature of urban life.

This intensified worries about the two-way link between the party and the urban working class. Forged in 1917, it had worn ever thinner. But it did not break asunder. The party developed its talent for persuasion, promotion and manipulation. Dozens of primers with titles such as *The ABC of Communism* explained the ultimate aims of Bolshevism. Poster art flourished.

Lenin the irreconcilable ended up as a symbol for reconcili-ation not only in the party but also more widely in society. The Politburo, being eager to suppress Russian nationalism, infil-trated and weakened any organisations – including the Ortho-dox Church – that might become a conduit for it. At the same time it was recognised that the style of rulership had to accom-modate itself to the traditions of the country. Peasants travelled to petition Lenin personally as once they had journeyed to the Romanov emperors. They did so on their own initiative and Lenin encouraged the practice. After his death in 1924 a cult of him was organised so that Lenin the atheist became the object of a quasi-religious veneration. Other state rituals too were fostered.

Annual processions and festivals celebrated occasions in the calendar associated with socialism. The 'Oktyabrina' ceremony, introduced to replace church christenings, was not widely successful. [164: *49*; 271: *99*]. The Bolshevik party understood that it was better that workers took to the streets for a holiday than that they were forbidden from massing in public at all which might make them resent the entire political order. Celebration was coupled with mobilisation. Cultural and sporting societies sprang up with state funding [237: *98, 110*]. The trade unions acquired nearly 10 million members by 1927 [85: *545*]. The Bolsheviks aimed to incorporate as many people as they could in organisations under the party's control.

Undoubtedly apathy and hostility were growing, but the party was not ineffective in sustaining the idea that a better world was in the making. Socialism of some kind remained a popular idea. Recurrent campaigns to recruit factory labourers into the party were conducted. By 1927, about 55 per cent of the membership

Cartoon 6   B. Uspenski's satirical comment from 1926 on the undemocratic political practices of the Bolsheviks.

'Hasn't the meeting finished yet?'
'Not yet, they're waiting for the chairman. He forgot the resolution and had to go home to fetch it!'

claimed working-class backgrounds [230: *116*]. Many newcomers, though, came from the urban lower middle class and were therefore suspect to the regime. This was true also of the composition of the state administration [207: *199*], and the Bolshevik central leaders worried that the old ruling classes were returning to power by stealth. Yet the counter-measures were impressive. A majority of state officials surveyed in 1926 and 1928 had not held posts under the Romanovs [269: *343*].

[x]   Moscow and the world in 1927

And yet from 1927 the NEP itself was in an advanced stage of dissolution. At first sight, this is baffling. The NEP had helped to reset the industrial and agricultural sectors on tracks of economic development, and the chances of further advance were sound. If the Bolsheviks merely matched the tsarist record in economic performance, in politics they were more ruthless and imaginative in reducing turmoil.

This failed to save them from troubles of their own. No Bolshevik leader in 1921 had envisaged the NEP otherwise than as a temporary retreat. Lenin came round, tentatively, to wanting to maintain the policy for a lengthy period, but he died without delineating a detailed strategy. Bukharin worked on Lenin's last thoughts and treated the NEP not as a retreat at all but as the occupation of a ridge from which to undertake the eventual ascent to socialism. Industrialisation and even collective farming could be fostered by the NEP [7: *177*]. Such a recasting of party policy had many critics in the party. In 1923, these formed the Left Opposition under the inspiration of Trotsky and E. A. Preobrazhenski. Intense factional conflict broke out. The Left Opposition, disdaining to make favourable comparisons of present and past, contrasted present with wished-for future. For all its vigour, moreover, the NEP had areas of debility. The mining enterprises in 1926 produced less than half of the 1913 amount. Armaments output lagged. The technological gap between the USSR and the major capitalist countries widened, particularly in the machine-tools sector. In agriculture, the size of the units of production still gave cause for concern. Kulaks were not 'big farmers' of a type familiar in the advanced capitalist countries; and in 1927 there were only 24,504 tractors in the Soviet republic [85: *945*]. International relations were acutely worrying, especially when the British Conservative cabinet broke off trade links in 1927. War scares had occurred earlier in the decade. The Left Opposition, asserting a Marxist analysis, contended that any success achieved by the NEP was ineluctably accompanied by an increase in the wealth of private traders and the better-off peasants. It also criticised the rise in urban unemployment and complained that in 1927 less than 1 per cent of the USSR's sown area belonged to collective farms [85: *940*].

The ascendant party leadership of Zinoviev, Kamenev, Stalin and Bukharin dismissed such arguments and the Left Opposition went down to heavy defeat in 1923–1924. Yet Zinoviev and Kamenev had already grown concerned about Stalin's growing power and about the consequences of the NEP, and in 1925 they established the Leningrad Opposition. Next year they allied with Trotsky in forming the United Opposition. Stalin and Bukharin refused to give an inch. By 1927 they had defeated the United Opposition and confirmed their dominance. Oppositionist activists either recanted or suffered expulsion from the party and, in some cases, administrative exile. The United Opposition had never had a general democratic platform. They wanted a Bolshevik party political monopoly as much as the other Bolsheviks did; and, though they talked of reintroducing internal democratic procedures to the party, the strength of their commitment was suspect. More open forms of decision making might anyway have induced more disruption than co-ordination [241: *197–8*]. It also beggars belief that richer peasants would have voluntarily acceded to the higher rates of taxation required for faster industrial capital accumulation or that the middling sections of the peasantry were persuadable to join collective farms.

Yet loyal party officials at the centre and in the localities, while rejecting the Opposition's political demands, shared their wish to accelerate the drive towards economic modernisation and military security – and Stalin was one of them. Their inclination was reinforced by each successive crisis, at home or abroad, that had to be endured. The NEP had few unembarrassed apologists like Bukharin. Already in the tax year 1925–1926 the ascendant party leadership was finding the itch to unsettle its own policy irresistible. A fiscal law was introduced discriminating heavily against the richer peasants in order to raise revenues for state industrial investment; and when pricing policy was mishandled for agricultural and industrial goods in 1927, grain marketing shrank. Simultaneously Gosplan, the state central planning agency, was being put under orders to draft a five-year plan for quicker industrialisation. By the end of 1927 there was yet another food supplies crisis. In January 1928 Stalin led an official contingent to the Urals and western Siberia and requisitioned grain by force. Financial experts who forecast chaos from the Five-Year Plan were silenced; and a show trial of engineers in Shakhty terrified managers and specialists throughout the country. Bukharin and his friends were dubbed 'rightist deviationists'; they did not have enough support in the party to merit being called an opposition [195: 53]. Industrial targets rose steeply. In order to secure food supplies as well as to boost grain exports and facilitate the purchase of foreign technology, Stalin's group resolved to use massive violence to push peasants into collective farms. Wanting to eliminate potential resistance, the Politburo denied permission for kulaks to stay on their land. Hundreds of thousands were shipped to Siberia. The terrorised peasantry, starving in the countryside by 1932, migrated in millions to the towns in search of work and food.

These lunges into forced-rate industrialisation and forcible agricultural collectivisation bring us to the boundaries of this account. At the end of the 1920s a transformation was put in motion which equalled the Revolution of 1917 in importance. Stalin had only a sketchy programme in mind at the outset of the First Five-Year Plan. Initially he and his associates blithely assumed they would raise the workers' material standard of living and provide most collective farms with tractors. Of such colossal miscalculations was the scheme to terminate the NEP composed.

Stalin was undertaking an act of will. In a century that produced not only him but also Hitler and Churchill, who would deny that individual politicians could make an egregious impact upon their times? Lenin too was a political giant. A multitude of decisions would never have been taken, or at least would have been formulated with substantial differences, if Lenin had not existed. Nonetheless neither Lenin nor Stalin could operate without organised backing. The ending of the NEP, in particular, was a perennial possibility throughout its time-span. The desire for a more closely administered society and economy was not peculiar to full-time party officials. Similar feelings were expressed inside the party's youth organisation and in the political police. In the educational establishment too voices were raised for radically new policies. Several literary groups spoke in similar fashion. At the same time there were murmurings of discontent in the factories that wages and conditions remained poor. The case is sometimes put that Stalin merely responded to these pressures. This is unconvincing. Rather it was the case that Stalin and his central associates deliberately used and magnified the pressures [248: 27]. Disenchantment with the NEP was not universal; and, where it existed, it was inchoate: and there was little consideration of exactly what should replace it.

Stalin and his associates gave the break in policy its shape. And, as the expansion of industry and education and administration gathered pace, so social mobility increased. Promotions were frequent. An increased number of people acquired an interest in the maintenance of the Soviet order. Thus the massive violence accompanying the remoulding of the Soviet state and its economy involved the cultivation of areas of social support. The year 1927 therefore was a historic landmark. It divided the unstable edifice of the first post-revolutionary decade from the years when a firm structure of state and society was erected in the USSR. This structure too had its strains and uncompleted sections but endured several decades. Its residual strength was demonstrated by the difficulty experienced by political leaderships when seeking to reform it in the decades after Stalin's death in 1953. But that is another story.

Conclusions

The Revolution of 1917 was a culmination and a beginning; an old order was ended, a new one inaugurated. The events were also an interruption. Economic achievement had been impressed before the First World War and was substantial again under the NEP. The social transformation initiated in the late Imperial period was resumed in the early 1920s. Both Nicholas II's government and the Bolsheviks enabled such modernisation. State economic intervention, which was not negligible before 1917, was massive thereafter. The thrust towards modernity was not generated exclusively by political action from on high. Society in general helped to create and sustain it. The Imperial authorities could never subject their people to anything near to close control, and their incapacity was growing from the start of the twentieth century. Only spasmodic repression was practicable. Subsequently the Bolsheviks, despite amassing greater resources for coercion, encountered resistance from sections of the working class and the peasantry in the Civil War; and concessions were an acute requirement by 1921. There were other continuities between the two regimes. Open political opposition was restricted severely under Nicholas II until 1905 and even more severely under Bolshevism. Abject poverty persisted widely. Ideological intolerance spanned the years before and after 1917. The country's basic requirements were constant. In the first decade of Bolshevik rule it remained as urgent to build up economic strength and military capacity as in the reigns of the last Romanov emperors. Although the pursuit of material progress gave positive results, it also accentuated points of weakness. Social tensions endured. Stable economic growth was frequently disrupted and agriculture in particular was susceptible to recurrent calamity.

The Imperial regime's inadequacies were exposed in 1905–1906, and the monarchy collapsed in February 1917 after the Great War had induced the final, crippling strain. What little agreement united the foes of tsarism quickly disappeared. Workers, soldiers and peasants were unwilling to accept most forms of authority associated with the old order. Their demands were initially ratified by the October seizure of power. Some gains were of a lasting nature. The promotion of workers to administrative posts commenced. Working-class pride was fostered and the property rights of the wealthy were eliminated. Peasants benefited from the removal of their landlords. Not all technical personnel were entirely displeased with the contrast between the governments of Lenin and Nicholas II. The Bolsheviks were more effective than Nicholas II and his ministers in imposing their monopoly of state authority.

The chances of the makers of the October Revolution moving along a route of peaceful, steady development were never great. The year 1917 gave rise to contradictory and unrealistic goals. This occurred against a background of economic collapse through to 1921, and scarcity of material goods nurtured strife. Cultural and social traditions also restricted the willingness – after the lull in spring 1917 – to settle public disputes peacefully; and the Bolsheviks, who were the product of such a society, widened the arena for political ruthlessness. The Civil War too had brutalising effects. Even in Lenin's lifetime crucial practical and theoretical restraints upon the scope of state power had been brusquely removed. And although the passage towards a still harsher form of the Soviet regime by the end of the 1920s was not unavoidable, it was always a strong possibility. Lenin had bequeathed a one-party, one-ideology state. He had retained terror as a method of rule. He and his associates had established the institutional instruments needed by Stalin to inaugurate his own even more terrifying form of communist dictatorship. He had classified the party's adversaries as enemies of the people and coarsened attitudes throughout society; and while compromising over aspects of economic organisation through his NEP, Lenin never intended his strategic retreat to be a permanent one [185: *299*].

But would Lenin have gone as far as Stalin in applying the methods of violence? This is doubtful. Lenin found the trappings of personal despotism uncongenial. He felt less insecure in party and government than Stalin did. If he had lived, he was unlikely to have executed or imprisoned millions of people who had not raised a hand against him and his policies. What Lenin might have done about the agricultural sector of the economy is not quite as clear; but there is little reason to suppose that violent mass collectivisation would have been his preferred option.

Lenin did not survive to deal with the problems – international, political, ethnic, cultural and economic problems – that became acute over the years of the NEP. Stalin's admirers always claimed that the Stalinist alternative was the sole realistic programme by the late 1920s. Thus, they argued, the early Five-Year Plans catapulted the USSR in the direction of a fuller industrial and technical modernisation; and the potential for the defeat of a mighty aggressor such as Nazi Germany came within range. But these successes must not dazzle our judgement. Forced-rate industrialisation and forcible agricultural collectivisation caused social torment. Stalin, moreover, exaggerated how much material improvement had come through his policies. It is not clear that the continuation of the NEP would necessarily have left the Soviet Union militarily helpless in 1941. Official spokesmen in the 1930s anyway ignored the progress already made in the later Imperial and early Soviet epochs; industrialisation was under way before Stalin's political ascendancy commenced. And the difficulties faced by later reformers, both Soviet and post-Soviet, in trying to introduce initiative, social fairness and legality to Russian society have stemmed from the Stalinist legacy. But if Lenin had not given him the map, Stalin would have never had the chance to select the destination.

Select Bibliography

General works

[1] E. Acton, *Rethinking the Russian Revolution* (London, 1990). Thought-ful review of historical writing about 1917 since the Second World War.

[2] E. Acton, V. Yu. Cherniaev and W. G. Rosenberg, *Critical Companion to the Russian Revolution, 1914–1921* (London, 1997). Compendium of perceptive articles, from Russia and abroad.

[3] V. Brovkin, *Behind the Front Lines of the Civil War: Political Parties and Social Movements in Russia, 1918–1922* (Princeton, NJ, 1994). Spirited argument that the Civil War was a series of very local military conflicts.

[4] V. Buldakov, *Krasnaya smuta: priroda i posledstviya revolyutsionnogo nasiliya* (Moscow, 1997). One of the first Russian textbooks that is equally critical of Soviet and Western accounts of the year 1917.

[5] V. Buldakov, *Quo Vadis? Krizisy v Rossii – puti pereosmysleniya* (Moscow, 2006). Extension of the author's arguments about 1917 to Russian history to the rest of the twentieth century.

[6] E. H. Carr, *The Bolshevik Revolution*, vols 1–3 (London, 1951–1953). Influential and still controversial account emphasising the impact of state interests upon Bolshevik revolutionary dreams.

[7] S. F. Cohen, *Bukharin and the Russian Revolution: A Political Biography, 1888–1938* (London, 1974). Eulogy of Bukharin as the would-be eliminator of dictatorial policies from Bolshevism after the Civil War.

[8] R. W. Davies (ed.), *From Tsarism to the New Economic Policy: Continuity and Change in the Economy of the USSR* (London, 1990). Rigorous survey of the economy across the dividing line of 1917.

[9] I. Deutscher, *The Unfinished Revolution* (Oxford, 1967). Vigorous case by a veteran Trotskyist for the inevitable degeneration of the October Revolution.

[10] M. Fainsod, *How Russia is Ruled* (Cambridge, MA, 1953).

[11] O. Figes, *A People's Tragedy: The Russian Revolution, 1891–1924* (London, 1996). Elegant narrative, told chiefly through the experiences of six main witnesses.

[12]   S. Fitzpatrick, *The Russian Revolution* (Oxford, 1982). Concise study of the first two decades after 1917, stressing the shaping impact of social aspirations.

[13]   P. Gatrell, *Russia's First World War: A Social and Economic History* (London, 2005).

[14]   P. Gatrell, *The Tsarist Economy, 1850–1917* (London, 1986). Thorough account of work on the pre-revolutionary economy.

[15]   A. Gerschenkron, *Economic Backwardness in Historical Perspective: A Book of Essays* (New York, 1965). The most influential statement of the positive potential of the economy before 1914.

[16]   T. Hasegawa, *The February Revolution: Petrograd, 1917* (London, 1981). Measured analysis of tsar, Duma, elites and masses in the February 1917 Revolution.

[17]   G. A. Hosking, *Russia: People and Empire* (London, 1997). Energetic account of the tension between the objectives of empire and the aspirations of the people through to 1917.

[18]   G. A. Hosking, *Rulers and Victims: The Russians in the Soviet Union* (London, 2006). Consideration of the privileges and disadvantages for the Russian people in the Soviet decades.

[19]   J. L. H. Keep, *The Russian Revolution: A Study in Mass Mobilisation* (London, 1976). Important study of the revolutionaries' manipulation of mass organisations in 1917–1918.

[20]   D. P. Koenker, W.G. Rosenberg and R. G. Suny, *Party, State and Society in the Russian Civil War: Explorations in Social History* (Bloomington, IN, 1988). Set of carefully researched essays on the Civil War.

[21]   M. Lewin, *Lenin's Last Struggle* (London, 1968). Provocative argument that Lenin's last writings pointed towards a reorientation of Bolshevism away from dictatorship and terror.

[22]   D. Lieven, *Russia and the Origins of the First World War* (London, 1983). Balanced analysis of the factors that shaped Imperial foreign policy.

[23]   M. Malia, 'Revolution Fulfilled: How The Revisionists Are Still Trying To Take The Ideology Out Of Stalinism', *Times Literary Supplement*, 15 June 2001. Review article covering two decades before the Second World War.

[24]   E. Mawdsley, *The Russian Civil War* (Boston, 1987). Systematic and clear account, blending military and political factors.

[25]   A. Nove, *Economic History of the USSR* (London, 1969). Still the most gripping survey of the economy and society in the revolutionary period and subsequently.

[26]   R. Pipes, *The Russian Revolution, 1899–1919* (London, 1990). Passionate account centred on Lenin's capacity to dominate, deceive and kill.

[27]   B. N. Ponomarëv and others (eds), *Istoriya Kommunisticheskoi Partii Sovetskogo Soyuza* (Moscow, 1985). Official party textbook on Soviet history, issued in several editions through to the Gorbachëv years.

[28]   P. N. Pospelov and others, *Vladimir Il'ich Lenin: biografiya* (Moscow, 1965). Last Soviet biography of Lenin, modified each subsequent year according to official political requirements.

[29] C. Read, *The Russian Revolution* (London, 1996). Meticulous compilation of the secondary literature on the Revolution, being particularly strong on the cultural aspects.

[30] L. B. Schapiro, *The Communist Party of the Soviet Union* (London, 1960). Classic account of communist history written in condemnation of Soviet legal nihilism.

[31] R. Service, *Comrades. Communism: A World History* (London, 2007). Account of modern communism around the world, its origins and impact.

[32] R. Service, *A History of Modern Russia: From Nicholas II to Putin* (London, 2003). Attempt to explain the Russian Revolution's origins, course and long-term outcome.

[33] R. Service (ed.), *Society and Politics in the Russian Revolution* (London, 1992). Collection of sober essays on attitudes and activity of large social groups in 1917.

[34] T. Shanin, *The Roots of Otherness: Russia's Turn of Century*, vols 1–2 (London, 1985–1986). Thought-provoking account asserting the durability and positive potential of Russian social institutions.

[35] H. Shukman (ed.), *The Blackwell Encyclopedia of the Russian Revolution* (Oxford, 1988). Handy collation of recent scholarship on the Russian Revolution.

[36] S. Smith, *The Russian Revolution: A Very Short Introduction* (Oxford, 2002). A general account, especially good on the 1920s.

[37] A. Solzhenitsyn, *August 1914* (London, 1983). Searing first volume in *The Red Wheel* sequence, which contends that the revolutions of 1917 resulted from malign forces alien to every decent Russian tradition.

[38] G. Swain, *Russia's Civil War* (Stroud, 2000). Succinct exposition of the interconnected political and military features of the fighting.

[39] P. V. Volobuev, *Vybor putei obshchestvennogo razvitiya: teoriya, istoriya, sovremennost'* (Moscow, 1987). Succinct critique of conventional Marxist-Leninist historical determinism by a leading 'reform-communist'.

Memoirs and contemporary analyses

[40] Otto Bauer, *Bolschewismus oder Sozialdemokratie?* (Vienna, 1920). Pioneering argument that the Russians got the revolution that their economic and social 'backwardness' determined. Long overdue for translation.

[41] N. Berdyaev, *The Russian Idea* (London, 1947). Influential account of the cultural receptiveness of Russians, after centuries of tsarism and Orthodox Christianity, to the kind of rule offered by the Bolsheviks.

[42] A. Blok, *The Twelve* in *Selected Poems* (London, 1974). Marvellous poem on 1917–1918 by the great poet who sympathised with the

Left Socialist-Revolutionaries and saw the popular revolutionary movement in its positive and negative aspects.

[43] W. H. Chamberlin, *The Russian Revolution, 1917–1921*, vols 1–2 (London, 1934). Still the greatest narrative history of the Russian Revolution written by a foreigner.

[44] V. Chernov, *The Great Russian Revolution* (London, 1936). Analytical and moving memoir by the leader of the Socialist-Revolutionaries in 1917.

[45] T. Dan, *The Origins of Bolshevism* (London, 1964). Steady critique of Bolshevik ideas by a Menshevik leader who, in his last years, took a surprisingly gentle approach to Stalin's rule.

[46] P. Dukes, *Red Dusk and the Morrow: Adventures and Investigations in Red Russia* (London, 1922).

[47] M. Eastman, *Since Lenin Died* (New York, 1925).

[48] K. Kautsky, *The Dictatorship of the Proletariat* (Ann Arbor, MI, 1964). Powerful denunciation of Bolshevik doctrine and strategy by a leading German Marxist.

[49] A. F. Kerensky, *The Crucifixion of Liberty* (London, 1934). Pungent memoir by the Provisional Government's last premier.

[50] Yu. Martov, *Mirovoi bol'shevizm* (Berlin, 1923). This study, *World Bolshevism*, by a leading Menshevik, is among the finest examinations of the ideological, political and social roots of the October Revolution. Alas, it remains untranslated into English.

[51] P. N. Milyukov, *The Russian* Revolution, vols 1–3 (Gulf Breeze, FL, 1978–1987). Sustained exposition of the defeat of Russian liberalism in 1917 and afterwards.

[52] B. Pasternak, *Doctor Zhivago* (London, 1957). Powerful novel on the Russian Revolution by one of Russia's great poets.

[53] J. Reed, *Ten Days that Shook the World* (London, 1977). Lively memoir by American journalist who took the Bolshevik side.

[54] B. Russell, *The Practice and Theory of Bolshevism* (London, 1920).

[55] P. Sorokin, *Leaves from a Russian Diary* (New York, 1924). Perceptive record by a Socialist-Revolutionary who became a distinguished sociologist in emigration.

[56] I. Steinberg, *In the Workshop of the Revolution* (London, 1955). Caustic memoir by a Left Socialist-Revolutionary who joined the Soviet government.

[57] N. Sukhanov, *The Russian Revolution* (Princeton, NJ, 1964). Abridged version of the massive account by Sukhanov, a left-wing Menshevik who knew all the party leaders in 1917. Still the greatest narrative history of the Revolution by a long way.

[58] L. Trotsky, *History of the Russian Revolution*, vols 1–3 (New York, 1932). Elegant, sardonic defence of the Bolshevik party in revolution.

[59] N. S. Trubetskoi, *K probleme russkogo samosoznaniya: sobranie statei* (Paris, 1927). Early statement of the Eurasianist interpretation of Russian history.

[60]   N. Ustryalov, *Pod znakom revolyutsii* (2nd revised edn: Harbin, 1920).
[61]   H. G. Wells, *Russia in the Shadows* (London, 1920).

Particular works

[62]   G. Alexopoulos, *Stalin's Outcasts: Aliens, Citizens, and the Soviet State, 1926–1936* (Ithaca, NY, 2003).
[63]   A. M. Anfimov, *Krupnoe pomeshchich'e khozyaistvo Evropeiskoi Rossii. (Konets XIX – nachalo XX veka)* (Moscow, 1969).
[64]   A. M. Anfimov and I. F. Makarov, 'Novye dannye o zemlevladenii Evropeiskoi Rossii', *Istoriya SSSR* (1974), no. 1.
[65]   A. Ascher, *The Revolution of 1905: Russia in Disarray* (Stanford, CA, 1988).
[66]   D. Atkinson, *The End of the Russian Land Commune, 1905–1930* (Stanford, CA, 1983).
[67]   J. Aves, *Workers Against Lenin: Labour Protest and the Bolshevik Dictatorship* (London, 1996).
[68]   A. Ya. Avrekh, *Tsarizm i IV-aya Duma, 1912–1914 gg.* (Moscow, 1981).
[69]   J. Baberowski, *Der Feind ist Überall: Stalinismus im Kaukasus* (Munich, 2003).
[70]   J. Baberowski, *Der Rote Terror: Die Geschichte des Stalinismus* (Munich, 2004).
[71]   S. Badcock, *Politics and the People in Revolutionary Russia: A Provincial History* (Cambridge, 2007).
[72]   P. Bairoch, 'Niveaux de développement économique de 1800 à 1910', *Annales* (November–December 1965).
[73]   A. M. Ball, *Russia's Last Capitalists: The Nepmen, 1921–1929* (Berkeley, CA, 1987).
[74]   A. Bennigsen and M. Broxup, *The Islamic Threat to the Soviet State* (London, 1983).
[75]   F. Benvenuti, *I Bolscevichi e L'Armata Rossa, 1918–1922* (Naples, 1983).
[76]   A. Blyum, *Za kulisami 'Ministerstva Pravdy': tainaya istoriya sovetskoi tsentsury* (St Petersburg, 1994).
[77]   V. Bonnell, *The Roots of Rebellion: Workers' Politics and Organisations in St Petersburg and Moscow, 1900–1914* (Berkeley, CA, 1983).
[78]   D. L. Brandenberger and A. M. Dubrovsky, '"The People Need a Tsar": The Emergence of National Bolshevism as Stalinist Ideology, 1931–1941', *Soviet Studies* (1998), no. 5.
[79]   J. Brooks, *When Russia Learned to Read: Literacy and Popular Literature, 1861–1917* (Princeton, NJ, 1985).
[80]   V. N. Brovkin, *The Mensheviks after the October Revolution: Socialist Opposition and the Rise of the Bolshevik Dictatorship* (Ithaca, NY, 1987).
[81]   V. Brovkin, *Russia After Lenin: Politics, Culture and Society* (London, 1998).

[82]   S. Brown, 'Communists and the Red Cavalry: Political Education of the *Konarmiya* in the Russian Civil War', *Slavonic and East European Review*, (1995), no. 1.

[83]   R. Brym and E. Economakis, 'Peasant or Proletarian: Militant Pskov Workers in St Petersburg, 1913', *Slavic Review* (1994), no. 1.

[84]   J. Bushnell, *Mutiny amid Repression: Russian Soldiers in the Revolution of 1905–1906* (Bloomington, IN, 1987).

[85]   E. H. Carr and R. W. Davies, *Foundations of a Planned Economy, 1926–1929*, vol. 1 (London, 1969).

[86]   L. Chamberlain, *The Philosophy Steamer: Lenin and the Exile of the Intelligentsia* (London, 2006).

[87]   J. D. Channon, 'The Bolsheviks and the Peasantry: The Land Question During the First Eight Months of Soviet Rule', *Slavonic and East European Review* (1988), no. 4.

[88]   W. J. Chase, *Workers, Society and the Soviet State: Labor and Life in Moscow, 1918–1929* (Urbana, IL, 1987).

[89]   O. Crisp, 'Labour and Industrialisation in Russia', *Cambridge Economic History of Europe*, vol. 7, part 2 (Cambridge, 1978).

[90]   O. Crisp, *Studies in the Russian Economy before 1914* (London, 1976).

[91]   V. P. Danilov, *Sovetskaya dokolkhoznaya derevnya: naselenie, zemlepol'zovanie, khozyaistvo* (Moscow, 1977).

[92]   V. P. Danilov, 'Sovetskaya nalogovaya politika v dokolkhoznoi derevne', in I. M. Volkov (ed.), *Oktyabr' i sovetskoe krest'yanstvo, 1917–1927 gg.* (Moscow, 1977).

[93]   V. P. Danilov, *Krest'yanskoe vosstanie v Tambovskoi gubernii, 1919–1921 gg. 'Antonovshchina'* (Moscow, 1994).

[94]   R. W. Davies, *The Development of the Soviet Budgetary System* (Cambridge, 1958).

[95]   R. W. Davies, *The Socialist Offensive: The Collectivisation of Soviet Agriculture, 1929–1930* (London, 1980).

[96]   R. W. Davies, 'Trotskij and the Debate on Industrialisation in the USSR', in F. Gori (ed.), *Pensiero e Azione Politica di Lev Trockij* (Florence, 1983), vol. 1.

[97]   M. Dewar, *Labour Policy in the USSR, 1917–1928* (London, 1956).

[98]   S. M. Dixon, 'The Russian Orthodox Church in Imperial Russia 1721–1917', in M. Angold (ed.), *The Cambridge History of Christianity*, vol. 5: *Eastern Christianity* (Cambridge, 2006).

[99]   M. Dobb, *Russian Economic Development since the Revolution* (London, 1928).

[100] V. Z. Drobizhev, *Glavnyi shtab sotsialisticheskoi promyshlennosti* (Moscow, 1966).

[101] V. Z. Drobizhev, A. K. Sokolov and V. A. Ustinov, *Rabochii klass Sovetskoi Rossii v pervyi god proletarskoi diktatury* (Moscow, 1975).

[102] S. M. Dubrovskii, *Sel'skoe khozyaistvo i krest'yanstvo Rossii v period imperializma* (Moscow, 1975).

[103] S. M. Dubrovskii, *Stolypinskaya zemel'naya reforma, Iz istorii sel'skogo khozyaistva i krest'yanstva Rossii v nachale XX veka* (Moscow, 1963).

[104] P. Dukes, 'October in the Mind: The Russian Revolution, *Freidizm* and Pandisciplinarity', *Revolutionary Russia* (2002), no. 1.

[105] C. Duval, 'Yakov M. Sverdlov and the All-Russian Central Executive Committee of Soviets (VTsIK): A Study in Bolshevik Consolidation of Power, October 1917–July 1918', *Soviet Studies* (1979), no. 1.

[106] V. S. Dyakin et al., *Krizis samoderzhaviya v Rossii, 1895–1917* (Leningrad, 1984).

[107] V. S. Dyakin, *Russkaya burzhuaziya i tsarizm v gody pervoi mirovoi voiny, 1914–1917* (Leningrad, 1967).

[108] R. Edelman, *Proletarian Peasants: The Revolution of 1905 in Russia's Southwest* (Ithaca, NY, 1987).

[109] R. C. Elwood, *Russian Social-Democracy In The Underground: A Study of the RSDRP in the Ukraine, 1907–1914* (Assen, 1974).

[110] T. Emmons, 'The Zemstvo in Historical Perspective', in T. Emmons (ed.) *The Zemstvo in Russia: An Experiment in Local Self-Government* (Cambridge, 1982).

[111] L. Engelstein, *The Keys to Happiness: Sex and the Search for Modernity in Fin-de-siècle Russia* (2nd edn: Ithaca, NY, 1996).

[112] M. E. Falkus, *The Industrialisation of Russia, 1700–1914* (London, 1972).

[113] M. Ferro, 'The Aspirations of Russian Society', in R. Pipes (ed.), *Revolutionary Russia* (Cambridge, MA, 1968).

[114] O. Figes and B. Kolonitskii, *Interpreting the Russian Revolution: The Language and Symbols of 1917* (London 1999).

[115] O. Figes, *Peasant Russia, Civil War, The Volga Countryside in Revolution, 1917–1921* (Oxford, 1989).

[116] S. Fitzpatrick, 'Ordzhonikidze's Takeover of Vesenkha: A Case Study in Soviet Bureaucratic Politics', *Soviet Studies* (1985), no. 2.

[117] S. Fitzpatrick, A. Rabinowitch and R. Stites (eds), *Russia in the Era of NEP: Explorations in Soviet Society and Culture* (Bloomington, IN, 1991).

[118] S. Fitzpatrick, 'Sex and Revolution: An Examination of Literacy and Statistical Data on the Mores of Soviet Students in the 1920s', *Journal of Modern History* (June 1978).

[119] T. Friedgut, *Iuzovka and Revolution*, vol. 2, *Politics and Revolution in Russia's Donbass* (Princeton, NJ, 1994).

[120] W. C. Fuller, Jr., *The Foe Within, Fantasies of Treason and the End of Imperial Russia* (Ithaca, NY, 2006).

[121] Z. Galili, *The Menshevik Leaders in the Russian Revolution: Social Realities and Political Strategies* (Princeton, NJ, 1989).

[122] L. S. Gaponenko, *Rabochii klass Rossii v 1917 godu* (Moscow, 1970).

[123] P. W. Gatrell, 'Industrial Expansion in Tsarist Russia, 1908–1914', *Economic History Review* (1982), no. 1.

[124] P. Gatrell, *A Whole Empire Walking: Refugee in Russia during World War I* (Bloomington, IN, 1999).

[125] A. Gerschenkron, 'Agrarian Policies and Industrialisation: Russia 1861–1917', *Cambridge Economic History of Europe*, vol. 6, part 2 (Cambridge, 1966).

[126] A. Gerschenkron, 'The Rate of Growth of Industrial Production in Russia since 1885', *Journal of Economic History* (1947), no. 7.

[127] I. Getzler, *Kronstadt, 1917–1921: The Fate of a Soviet Democracy* (Cambridge, 1983).

[128] G. Gill, *Peasants and Government in the Russian Revolution* (London, 1979).

[129] E. V. Gimpel'son, *Velikii Oktyabr' i stanovlenie sovetskoi sistemy upravleniya narodnym khozyaistvom (noyabr' 1917–1920 gg.)* (Moscow, 1977).

[130] E. V. Gimpel'son, *'Voennyi kommunizm'; politika, praktika, ideologiya* (Moscow, 1973).

[131] I. A. Gladkov, *Sovetskoe narodnoe khozyaistvo v 1921–1925 gg.* (Moscow, 1960).

[132] R. Glickman, 'The Russian Factory Woman, 1880–1914', in D. Atkinson, A. Dallin and G. Warshofsky Lapidus (eds), *Women in Russia* (Stanford, CA, 1977).

[133] A. Gorsuch, *Flappers and Foxtrotters: Soviet Youth in the Roaring Twenties* (Pittsburgh, PA, 1994).

[134] P. Gregory, 'Economic Growth and Structural Change in Tsarist Russia: A Case of Modern Economic Growth?', *Soviet Studies* (December 1967).

[135] P. Gregory, *Before Command: The Russian Economy From Emancipation to Stalin* (Princeton, NJ, 1994).

[136] P. Gregory, *Russian National Income, 1885–1913* (Cambridge, 1982).

[137] M. von Hagen, *Soldiers in the Proletarian Dictatorship: the Red Army and the Soviet Socialist State, 1917–1930* (Ithaca, NY, 1990).

[138] L. H. Haimson, 'The Problem of Urban Stability in Russia, 1905–1917', *Slavic Review* (1964), no. 5 and (1965), no. 1.

[139] G. M. Hamburg, *Politics of the Russian Nobility, 1881–1905* (New Brunswick, NJ, 1984).

[140] N. Harding, *Lenin's Political Thought* (London, 1981), vol. 2.

[141] J. W. Heinzen, *Inventing a Soviet Countryside: State Power and the Transformation of Rural Russia* (Pittsburg, PA, 2004).

[142] M. Hildermeier, *Die Sozialrevolutionäre Partei Russlands: Agrarsozialismus und Modernisierung im Zarenreich (1900–1914)* (Cologne-Vienna, 1976).

[143] H. Hogan, 'The Reorganisation of Work Processes in the St Petersburg Metal-working Industry, 1901–14', *Russian Review* (1983), no. 2.

[144] P. Holquist, *Making War, Forging Revolution: Russia's Continuum of Crisis, 1914–1921* (London, 2002).

[145] G. A. Hosking, *The Russian Constitutional Experiment: Government and Duma, 1907–1914* (Cambridge, 1973).

[146] R. E. Johnson, *Peasant and Proletarian: The Working Class of Moscow in the Late Nineteenth Century* (Leicester, 1979).

[147] V. V. Kabanov, *Krest'yanskoe khozyaistvo v usloviyakh 'voennogo kommunizma'* (Moscow, 1988).

[148] V. V. Kabanov, 'Oktyabr'skaya revolyutsiya i krest'yanskaya obshchina', *Istoricheskie zapiski* (1984), vol. 111.

[149] A. Kahan, 'Capital Formation During the Period of Early Industrialisation in Russia, 1890–1913', *Cambridge Economic History of Europe*, vol. 7, part 2 (Cambridge, 1978).

[150] N. Kakurin, *Strategicheskii ocherk Grazhdanskoi voiny* in N. Kakurin, N. Kovtun and V. Sukhov, *Voennaya istoriya Grazhdanskoi voiny v Rossii, 1918–1920gg.* (Moscow, 2004).

[151] S. Karsch, *Die bolschewistische Machtergreifung im Gouvernment Voronež (1917–1919)* (Stuttgart, 2006).

[152] E. M. Kayden and A. N. Antsiferov, *The Co-operative Movement in Russia During The War* (New Haven, CT, 1929).

[153] C. Kelly, *Children's World: Growing up in Russia 1800–1991* (London, 2007).

[154] C. Kelly, *Refining Russia: Advice Literature, Polite Culture, and Gender from Catherine to Yeltsin* (Oxford, 2001).

[155] P. Kenez, 'A Profile of the Pre-Revolutionary Officer Corps', *California Slavic Studies* (1973), no. 7.

[156] P. A. Khromov, *Ekonomicheskoe razvitie Rossii: Ocherki ekonomiki Rossii s drevneishikh vremen do Velikoi Oktyabr'skoi revolyutsii* (Moscow, 1967).

[157] A. Khryashcheva, *Krest'yanstvo v voine i revolyutsii* (Moscow, 1921).

[158] C. Kiaer and E. Naiman (eds) *Everyday Life in Early Soviet Russia* (Bloomington, IN, 2006).

[159] T. Kitanina, *Khlebnaya torgovlya Rossii, 1875–1914 gg. (Ocherki pravitel'stvennoi politiki)* (Leningrad, 1978).

[160] T. M. Kitanina, *Voina, khleb i revolyutsiya: prodovol'stvennyi vopros v Rossii, 1914–oktyabr' 1917 g.* (Leningrad, 1985).

[161] Yu. I. Kir'yanov, *Zhiznennyi uroven' rabochikh Rossii (konets XIX–nachalo XX vv.)* (Moscow, 1979).

[162] J. Klier, 'The Pogrom Paradigm in Russian History', in J. Klier and S. Lambroza (eds), *Pogroms: Anti-Jewish Violence in Modern Russian History* (Cambridge, 1992).

[163] S. M. Klyatskin, *Na zashchite Oktyabrya: Organizatsiya regulyarnoi armii i militsionnoe stroitel'stvo v Sovetskoi respublike, 1917–1920* (Moscow, 1965).

[164] D. Koenker, 'Class Consciousness in a Socialist Society', in S. Fitzpatrick, A. Rabinowitch and R. Stites (eds), *Russia in the Era of the NEP: Explorations in Soviet Society and Culture* (Bloomington, IN, 1991).

[165] D. Koenker, *Moscow Workers and the 1917 Revolution* (Princeton, NJ, 1981).

[166] B. Kolonitskii, *Simvoly vlasti i bor'ba za vlast': k izucheniyu politicheskoi kul'tury rossiiskoi revolyutsii 1919 goda* (St. Petersburg, 2001).

[167] D. Kol'tsov, 'Rabochie v 1890–1904 gg.', in L. Martov, P. Maslov and A. Potresov (eds), *Obshchestvennoe dvizhenie v Rossii v nachale XX-go veka*, vol. 1 (St Petersburg, 1909).

[168] A. P. Korelin, *Dvoryanstvo poreformennoi Rossii, 1861–1905 gg.* (Moscow, 1979).

[169] I.D. Koval'chenko, 'Sootnosheniekrest'yanskogoipomeshchich'ego khozyaistva v zemlevladel'cheskom proizvodstve kapitalisticheskoi Rossii', in L. I. Ivanov et al. (eds), *Problemy sotsial'no-ekonomicheskoi istorii Rossii: Sbornik statei* (Moscow, 1971).

[170] N. A. Kravchuk, *Massovoe krest'yanskoe dvizhenie v Rossii nakanune Oktyabrya (mart-oktyabr' 1917g.): Po materialam velikorusskikh gubernii Evropeiskoi Rossii* (Moscow, 1971).

[171] E. E. Kruze, *Polozhenie rabochego klassa Rossii v 1900–1914 gg.* (Leningrad, 1976).

[172] H. Kuromiya, *Freedom and Terror in the Donbas: A Ukrainian-Russian Borderland, 1870s–1990s* (Cambridge, 1998).

[173] S. Lambroza, 'The Pogroms of 1903–1906', in J. Klier and S. Lambroza (eds), *Pogroms: Anti-Jewish Violence in Modern Russian History* (Cambridge, 1992).

[174] L. Lande, 'Some Statistics of the Unification Congress, August 1917' in L. H. Haimson (ed.), *The Mensheviks from the Revolution of 1917 to the Second World War* (Chicago, IL, 1974).

[175] I. Lauchlan, *Russian Hide-and-Seek: The Tsarist Secret Police in St. Petersburg, 1906–1914* (Helsinki, 2002).

[176] V. Ya. Laverychev, *Gosudarstvo i monopolii v dorevolyutsionnoi Rossii* (Moscow, 1982).

[177] G. Leggett, *The Cheka: Lenin's Political Police. The All-Russian Extraordinary Commission for Combating Counter-Revolution and Sabotage (December 1917 to February 1922)* (Oxford, 1981).

[178] D. Lieven, *Nicholas II: Emperor of All the Russias* (London, 1993).

[179] D. Lieven, 'The Russian Civil Service under Nicholas II: Some Variations on the Bureaucratic Theme', *Jahrbücher für Geschichte Osteuropas* (1981), no. 29.

[180] L. Lih, *Bread and Authority in Russia, 1914–1921* (Berkeley, CA, 1990).

[181] U. Liszkowski, *Zwischen Liberalismus und Imperialismus: Die zaristische Aussenpolitik vor dem Ersten Weltkrieg im Urteil Miljukovs und der Kadetten-partei, 1905–1914* (Stuttgart, 1974).

[182] E. Lohr, *Nationalizing the Russian Empire: The Campaign Against Enemy Aliens during World War I* (Cambridge, MA, 2003).

[183] G. Lonergan, 'Resistance, Support and the Changing Dynamics of the Village in Kolchakia in the Russian Civil War', *Revolutionary Russia* (2008), no. 1.

[184] F. Lorimer, *The Population of the Soviet Union: History And Prospects* (Geneva, 1946).

[185] H. D. Löwe, *Die Lage der Bauern in Russland, 1880–1905: Wirtschafliche und soziale Veränderungen in der ländlichen Gesellschaft des Zarenreiches* (St. Katherinen, 1987).

[186] A. Luukanen, *The Party of Unbelief: The Religious Policy of the Bolshevik Party, 1917–1929* (Helsinki, 1994).

[187] S. Lyandres, 'On the Problem of "Indecisiveness" Among the Duma Leaders During the February Revolution: The Imperial

Decree of Prorogation and Decision to Convene the Private Meeting of 27 February 1917', *The Soviet and Post-Soviet Review*, nos 1–2 (1997).

[188] R. B. MacKean, *St. Petersburg between the Revolutions. Workers and Revolutionaries, June 1907 to February 1917* (New Haven, CT, 1990).

[189] D. Mandel, *The Petrograd Workers and the Fall of the Old Regime* (London, 1983).

[190] R. T. Manning, *The Crisis of the Old Order in Russia: Gentry and Government* (Princeton, NJ, 1982).

[191] J. E. Marot, 'Class Conflict, Political Competition and Social Transformation: Critical Perspectives on the Social History of the Russian Revolution', *Revolutionary Russia* (1994), no. 2.

[192] T. Martin, *The Affirmative Action Empire: Nationalism in the Soviet Union 1923–1939* (Ithaca, NY, 2001).

[193] E. Mawdsley, *The Russian Revolution and the Baltic Fleet: War and Politics, February 1917–April 1918* (London, 1984).

[194] M. Melancon, *The Lena Goldfields Massacre and the Crisis of the Late Tsarist State* (Austin, TX, 2006).

[195] C. Merridale, *Moscow Politics and the Rise of Stalin* (London, 1990).

[196] C. Merridale, *Night of Stone: Death and Memory in Russia* (London, 2000).

[197] S. Merl, *Der Agrarmarkt und die Neue Ökonomische Politik: Die Anfänge staatlicher Lenkung der Landwirtschaft in der Sowjetunion 1925–1928* (Munich-Vienna, 1981).

[198] M. A. Miller, *Freud and the Bolsheviks: Psychoanalysis in Imperial Russia and the Soviet Union* (New Haven, CT, 1998).

[199] S. Milligan, 'The Petrograd Bolsheviks and Social Insurance, 1914–1917', *Soviet Studies* (1968–9), no. 3.

[200] I. I. Mints, *Istoriya velikogo Oktyabrya*, vol. 1, *Sverzhenie samoderzhaviya* (Moscow, 1967).

[201] D. Moon, *The Russian Peasantry, 1600–1930: The World the Peasants Made* (London, 1999).

[202] W. Mosse, 'Revolution in Saratov (October–November 1917)', *Slavonic and East European Review* (October 1981).

[203] R. Munting, 'A Note on Gentry Landownership in European Russia', *New Zealand Slavonic Journal* (1978), no. 1.

[204] N. M. Naimark, *Terrorists and Social Democrats: The Russian Revolutionary Movement Under Alexander III* (Cambridge, MA, 1983).

[205] J. Neuberger, *Hooliganism: Crime, Culture and Power in St Petersburg, 1900–1914* (Berkeley, CA, 1993).

[206] A. S. Nifontov, *Zernovoe proizvodstvo Rossii vo vtoroi polovine XIX veka* (Moscow, 1974).

[207] D. Orlovsky, 'State Building in the Civil War Era: the Role of the Lower-Middle Strata', in D. P. Koenker, W. G. Rosenberg and R. G. Suny (eds), *Party, State and Society in the Russian Civil War: Explorations in Social History* (Bloomington, IN, 1989).

[208] T. V. Osipova, 'Razvitie sotsialisticheskoi revolyutsii v derevne v pervyi god diktatury proletariata', in I. M. Volkov et al. (eds), *Oktyabr' i sovetskoe krest'yanstvo, 1917–1922 gg.* (Moscow, 1977).

[209] J. Pallot, 'Agrarian Modernization on Peasant Farms in the Era of Capitalism', in J. H. Bater and R. A. French (eds), *Studies in Russian Historical Geography*, vol. 2 (London, 1983).

[210] R. Pearson, *The Russian Moderates and the Crisis of Tsarism, 1914–1917* (London, 1977).

[211] N. G. O. Pereira, *White Siberia: The Politics of Civil War* (Montreal, 1996).

[212] M. Perrie, *The Agrarian Policy of the Russian Socialist-Revolutionary Party from its Origins through the Revolution of 1905–1907* (Cambridge, 1976).

[213] R. Pethybridge, *The Social Prelude To Stalinism* (London, 1974).

[214] S. Pirani, *The Russian Revolution in Retreat, 1920–24: Soviet Workers and the New Communist Elite* (London, 2008).

[215] Yu. A. Polyakov, *Perekhod k nepu i sovetskoe krest'yanstvo* (Moscow, 1967).

[216] A. Pospielovsky, 'Strikes During the NEP', *Revolutionary Russia* (1997) no. 1.

[217] M. Pushkin, 'Raznochintsy in the University: Government Policy and Social Change in Nineteenth Century Russia', *International Review of Social History* (1981), part 1.

[218] A. Rabinowitch, *The Bolsheviks Come to Power* (New York, 1976).

[219] A. Rabinowitch, *The Bolsheviks in Power: The First Year of Soviet Rule in Petrograd* (Bloomington, IN, 2007).

[220] A. Rabinowitch, 'The Evolution of the Local Soviets in Petrograd, November 1917–June 1918', *Slavic Review* (1987), no. 1.

[221] O. H. Radkey, *The Agrarian Foes of Communism. Promise and Default of the Russian Socialist-Revolutionaries, February to October 1917* (New York, 1958).

[222] O. H. Radkey, *The Election to the Russian Constituent Assembly of 1917* (Cambridge, MA, 1950).

[223] D. J. Raleigh, *Experiencing Russia's Civil War: Politics, Society and Revolutionary Culture in Saratov, 1917–1922* (Princeton, NJ, 2002).

[224] D. J. Raleigh, 'A Provincial Kronstadt: Popular Unrest in Saratov at the end of the Civil War', in D. J. Raleigh (ed.), *Provincial Landscapes: Local Dimensions of Soviet Power* (Pittsburgh, PA, 2001).

[225] D. J. Raleigh, 'Revolutionary Politics in Provincial Russia: The Tsaritsyn "Republic" in 1917', *Slavic Review* (summer 1981).

[226] D. J. Raleigh, *Revolution on the Volga: 1917 in Saratov* (Ithaca, NY, 1986).

[227] A. G. Rashin, 'Dinamika promyshlennykh kadrov SSSR za 1917-1958 gg.', in D. A. Baevskii (ed.), *Izmeneniya v chislennosti i sostave Sovetskogo rabochego klassa* (Moscow, 1961).

Select Bibliography

[228] A. G. Rashin, *Formirovanie rabochego klassa Rossii: Istoriko-ekonomicheskie ocherki* (Moscow, 1958).

[229] A. G. Rashin, *Naselenie Rossii za 100 let* (Moscow, 1956).

[230] I. S. Rat'kovskii, *Krasnyi terror i deyatel'nost' VChK v 1918 godu* (St. Petersburg, 2006).

[231] C. Read, *Culture and Power in Revolutionary Russia: The Intelligentsia and the Transition from Tsarism to Communism* (London, 1990).

[232] E. A. Rees, *State Control in Soviet Russia. The Rise and Fall of the Workers' and Peasants' Inspectorate, 1920–1934* (London, 1987).

[233] A. J. Rieber, *Merchants and Entrepreneurs in Imperial Russia* (Chapel Hill, NC, 1982).

[234] T. H. Rigby, *Communist Party Membership in the USSR, 1917–1967* (Princeton, NJ, 1968).

[235] T. H. Rigby, 'The First Proletarian Government', *British Journal of Political Science* (January 1974).

[236] T. H. Rigby, *Lenin's Government: Sovnarkom, 1917–1922* (Cambridge, 1979).

[237] J. Riordan, *Sport in Soviet Society: Development of Sport and Physical Education in Russia and the USSR* (Cambridge, 1977).

[238] H. Rogger, *Russia in the Age of Modernisation and Revolution, 1881–1917* (London, 1983).

[239] W. G. Rosenberg, 'Autonomous Politics and Locations of Power: Social History and the Question of Outcomes in 1917: A Response to John Marot', *Revolutionary Russia* (1996), no. 1.

[240] W. G. Rosenberg, *Liberals in the Russian Revolution: The Constitutional Democratic Party, 1917–1921* (Princeton, NJ, 1974).

[241] W. G. Rosenberg, 'Russian Labor and Bolshevik Power after October', *Slavic Review*, 44 (Summer 1985).

[242] J. Rossman, *Worker Resistance Under Stalin: Class and Revolution on the Shop Floor* (Cambridge, MA, 2005).

[243] R. Sakwa, *Soviet Communists in Power: A Study of Moscow during the Civil War, 1918–21* (London, 1988).

[244] J. Sanborn, *Drafting the Russian Nation: Military Conscription, Total War and Mass Politics, 1905–1925* (DeKalb, IL, 2003).

[245] R. Service, *The Bolshevik Party in Revolution: A Study in Organisational Change, 1917–1923* (London, 1979).

[246] R. Service, 'From Polyarchy to Hegemony: The Party's Role in the Construction of the Central Institutions of the Soviet State, 1917–1919', *Sbornik* (1984), no. 10.

[247] R. Service, 'The Industrial Workers', in R. Service (ed.), *Society and Politics in the Russian Revolution* (London, 1992).

[248] R. Service, 'Joseph Stalin: The Making of a Stalinist', in J. Channon (ed.), *Politics, Society and Stalinism in the USSR* (London, 2004).

[249] R. Service, *Lenin: A Political Life*, Vol. 2, *Worlds in Collision* (London, 1991).

[250] R. Service, *Lenin: A Political Life*, Vol. 3, *The Iron Ring* (London, 1995).

[251] R. Service, *Stalin: A Biography* (London, 2004).

[252] H. Seton-Watson, *The Russian Empire, 1801–1917* (Oxford, 1976).

[253] G. N. Sevast'yanov et al. (eds), '*Sovershenno sekretno': Lubyanka – Stalinu o polozhenii v strane (1922–1934 gg.)*, vol. 4, part 2 (Moscow, 2001).

[254] T. Shanin, *The Awkward Class: Political Sociology of Peasantry in a Developing Society: Russia, 1910–1925* (Oxford, 1972).

[255] D. Shearer, *Industry, State and Society in Stalin's Russia, 1926–1934* (Ithaca, NY, 1996).

[256] V. Shevzov, *Russian Orthodoxy on the Eve of Revolution* (Oxford, 2003).

[257] L. H. Siegelbaum, *Soviet State and Society between Revolutions, 1917–1929* (Cambridge, 1992).

[258] J. Y. Simms, 'The Crisis in Russian Agriculture at the End of the Nineteenth Century: A Different View', *Slavic Review* (1977), no. 3.

[259] Y. Slezkine, *The Jewish Century* (Princeton, NJ, 2004).

[260] J. D. Smele, *Civil War in Siberia: The Anti-Bolshevik Government of Admiral Kolchak, 1918–1920* (Cambridge, 1996).

[261] J. Smith, *The Bolsheviks and the National Question 1917–23* (London, 1999).

[262] M. Smith, 'War, Autocracy and Public Men: Grain Procurement and Politics, 1914–1917', unpublished research seminar paper (CREES, Birmingham, n.d.).

[263] S. Smith, *Red Petrograd: Revolution in the Factories, 1917–1918* (Cambridge, 1983).

[264] S. Smith, 'Rethinking the Autonomy of Politics in the Russian Revolution of 1917: A Reply to John Eric Marot', *Revolutionary Russia* (1995) no. 1.

[265] S. Smith, 'Writing the History of the Russian Revolution after the Fall of Communism', *Europe-Asia Studies* (1994), no. 4.

[266] Yu. B. Solov'ëv, *Samoderzhavie i dvoryanstvo v kontse XIX-go veka* (Leningrad, 1973).

[267] J. D. Sontag, 'Tsarist Debts and Tsarist Foreign Policy', *Slavic Review* (1968), no. 4.

[268] M. Steinberg, 'The Language of Popular Revolution', in M. Steinberg, *Voices of Revolution, 1917* (London 2001).

[269] S. Sternheimer, 'Administration for Development: The Emerging Bureaucratic Elite, 1920–1930', in W. K. Pintner and D. K. Rowney, *Russian Officialdom: The Bureaucratisation of Russian Society from the Seventeenth to the Twentieth Century* (London, 1980).

[270] R. Stites, 'Bolshevik Ritual Building in the 1920s', in S. Fitzpatrick, A. Rabinowitch and R. Stites (eds), *Russia in the Era of the NEP: Explorations in Soviet Society and Culture* (Bloomington, IN, 1991).

[271] R. Stites, *Revolutionary Dreams: Utopian Vision and Experimental Life in the Russian Revolution* (Oxford, 1989).

[272] H. Stone, 'The Soviet Government and Moonshine, 1917–1929', *Cahiers du Monde Russe et Soviétique* (1986), no. 3/4.

Select Bibliography

[273] N. Stone, *The Eastern Front, 1914–1917* (London, 1975).
[274] R. G. Suny, *The Baku Commune, 1917–1918: Class and Nationality in the Russian Revolution* (Princeton, NJ, 1972).
[275] R. G. Suny, 'Revision and Retreat in the Historiography of 1917: Social History and Its Critics', *Russian Review* (1994), no. 2.
[276] A. C. Sutton, *Western Technology and Soviet Economic Development 1917–1930* (Stanford, CA, 1968).
[277] G. Swain, *The Origins of the Russian Civil War* (London, 1996).
[278] G. Swain, *Russian Social-Democracy and the Legal Labour Movement, 1906–1914* (London, 1983).
[279] T. Swietochowski, *Russian Azerbaijan, 1905–1920: The Shaping of a National Identity in a Muslim Community* (Cambridge, 1985).
[280] Y. Taniuchi, *The Village Gathering in Russia in the mid-1920s* (Birmingham, 1968).
[281] R. Taylor, *The Politics of the Soviet Cinema, 1917–1929* (Cambridge, 1979).
[282] *Tret'ya vserossiiskaya konferentsiya professional'nykh soyuzov, 3-11 iyulya (20–28 iyunya st. st.) 1917 goda. Stenograficheskii otchet* (ed. D. Koenker: New York-London, 1982).
[283] P. Vinogradoff and M. T. Florinsky (eds), *The Economic and Social History of the World War: Russian Series*, (New Haven, CT, 1929–32), vols. 1–12.
[284] L. Viola, *Peasant Rebels under Stalin: Collectivization and the Culture of Peasant Resistance* (New York, 1996).
[285] P. V. Volobuev, *Ekonomicheskaya politika Vremennogo pravitel'stva* (Moscow, 1962).
[286] P. V. Volobuev (ed.), *Revolyutsiya i chelovek* (Moscow, 1997): V. V. Kanishchev, 'Prisoblenie radi vyzhivaniya (Meshchanskoe bytie epokhi 'voennogo kommunizma').
[287] *Vos'maya konferentsiya konferentsiya RKP(b), dekabr' 1919 goda. Protokoly* (Moscow, 1961).
[288] R. A. Wade, 'The Rajonnye Sovety of Petrograd: The Role of Local Political Bodies in the Russian Revolution', *Jahrbücher für Geschichte Osteuropas* (1972), no. 2.
[289] R. A. Wade, *The Russian Search for Peace, February–October 1917* (Stanford, CA, 1967).
[290] P. Waldron, *Between Two Revolutions: Stolypin and the Politics of Renewal in Russia* (London, 1997).
[291] P. Waldron, *Governing Tsarist Russia* (London, 2007).
[292] P. Waldron, 'States of Emergency: Autocracy and Extraordinary Legislation, 1881–1917', *Revolutionary Russia* (1995), no. 1.
[293] C. Ward, *Russia's Cotton Workers and the New Economic Policy: Shop-Floor Culture and State Policy, 1921–1929* (Cambridge, 1990).
[294] S. G. Wheatcroft, 'Famine and Epidemic Crises in Russia, 1918–1922: The Case of Saratov', *Annales de Démographie Historique* (1983).
[295] S. G. Wheatcroft, 'Grain Production and Utilisation in Russia and the USSR before Collectivisation', unpublished Ph.D. thesis (University of Birmingham, 1980).

[296] S. G. Wheatcroft, 'The Balance of Grain Production and Utilisation in Russia before and during the Revolution', unpublished research seminar paper (CREES, Birmingham, 1982).

[297] S. G. Wheatcroft, 'The Use of Meteorological Data to Supplement and Analyse Data on Grain Yields in Russia and the USSR, 1883–1950', unpublished research seminar paper (Cambridge, 1982).

[298] S. G. Wheatcroft, R. W. Davies and J. M. Cooper, 'Soviet Industrialisation Reconsidered: Some Preliminary Conclusions about Economic Developments between 1926 and 1941', *Economic History Review* (1986), no. 2.

[299] H. J. White, 'The Provisional Government and the Problem of Power in the Provinces, March-October 1917', unpublished Study Group on the Russian Revolution conference paper (January 1982).

[300] A. Wildman, *The End of the Russian Imperial Army: The Old Army and the Soldiers' Revolt (March–October 1917)* (Princeton, NJ, 1980).

[301] A. Wood, 'Siberian Exile in Tsarist Russia', *History Today* (September 1980).

[302] R. Wortman, *Scenarios of Power: Myth and Ceremony in Russian Monarchy*, vol. 2, *From Alexander II to the Abdication of Nicholas II*, (Princeton, NJ, 2000).

[303] I. A. Yurkov, *Ekonomicheskaya politika partii v derevne, 1917–1920* (Moscow, 1980).

[304] P. A. Zaionchkovskii, *Krizis samoderzhaviya na rubezhe 1870–1880 gg.* (Moscow, 1964).

[305] E. Zaleski, *Planning for Economic Growth in the Soviet Union, 1918–1932* (Chapel Hill, NC, 1971).

Chronology of Events

The events listed below are given according to the calendar in official Russian usage at the time.

1894	Nicholas II accedes to the Imperial throne. Signature of Franco-Russian alliance
1896	Khodynka Field disaster
1897	Ruble put on the gold standard
1898	Russian Social-Democratic Workers' Party is founded
1901	Party of Socialist-Revolutionaries is founded
1902	Foundation of the Union of Liberation, which in 1906 becomes the Constitutional-Democratic Party
1904	Removal of much anti-peasant legal discrimination
1904–5	Russo-Japanese War
1905	
January	'Bloody Sunday': peaceful demonstration is fired upon outside Winter Palace
October	Intensified strike movement; Nicholas II gives way and issues the October Manifesto
December	Moscow uprising is quelled
1906	
January	Promulgation of the Fundamental Law
April	Opening of the First State Duma
July	Dissolution of the Duma
1907	
February	Opening of the Second State Duma
June	Dissolution of the Duma and announcement of more restrictive electoral rules

November 1912	Third State Duma is elected
April	Lena gold fields massacre
November 1914	Fourth State Duma is opened
June	Street demonstrations in Petrograd
August 1915	Outbreak of First World War
April	Tsarist government signs secret treaties with its wartime Allies
May	War-industry committees are created
August 1916	Nicholas II becomes Commander-in-Chief. Progressive Block is formed
June	Brusilov's successful offensive on the Eastern front
December 1917	Murder of Rasputin. Guchkov sounds out generals about attempting a *coup d'état*
February	Workers strike and soldiers mutiny in Petrograd. The Petrograd Soviet is created
March	Nicholas II abdicates and the Provisional Government is established under Lvov. Spread of soviets. Peasants begin to exert pressure on landlords. Mensheviks and Socialist-Revolutionaries give the Provisional Government their conditional support
April	Lenin returns from Switzerland and publishes his *April Theses*. Milyukov's note to Allies provokes street demonstration in Petrograd. Milyukov and Guchkov resign from cabinet
May	Lvov forms coalition ministry involving Mensheviks and Socialist-Revolutionaries
June	First All-Russia Congress of Soviets of Workers' and Soldiers' Deputies. Russian military offensive on Eastern front. Proposal to grant regional autonomy to Ukraine
July	Resignation of Kadet ministers. Armed demonstration of workers and sailors in Petrograd. Lenin flees. Kerenski becomes premier

August	State Conference in Moscow. Germans take Riga. Kornilov mutiny is suppressed
September	Bolsheviks take over the Petrograd Soviet. Democratic Conference in Petrograd
October	Bolshevik Central Committee, cajoled by Lenin, decides to seize power. The Second All-Russia Congress of Soviets; overthrow of the Provisional Government and the establishment of Sovnarkom. Issuance of revolutionary decrees: on Peace, on Land, on the Press. Arrests of Kadets and others
November	Left Socialist-Revolutionaries definitively form own party. Constituent Assembly elections. Ceasefire on Eastern front
December	Extraordinary Commission (Cheka) is formed. Left Socialist-Revolutionaries join Sovnarkom. Banks are nationalised. Soviet forces invade Ukraine and Ukrainian Soviet government is announced
1918	
January	Opening and dispersal of the Constituent Assembly. Sovnarkom decides to form Red Army. Bolsheviks dispute the proposal for a separate peace with Central Powers
February	Basic Law on the land is introduced
March	Bolsheviks rename themselves as the Russian Communist party (Bolsheviks). Treaty of Brest-Litovsk: Russia withdraws from the First World War and renounces claims over the territory of Ukraine, Belorussia, Lithuania, Latvia and Estonia. Bolsheviks defeated in several Russian town soviets
April	Germans establish puppet regime of Skoropadsky in Ukraine
May	Czechoslovak Legion revolts
June	Socialist-Revolutionary government is formed in Samara. Massive campaign of industrial nationalisation. Decree on the committees of the village poor
July	Suppression of the Party of Left Socialist-Revolutionaries. Romanov family shot in the Urals
August	Assassination attempt on Lenin
September	Red Terror is formally proclaimed. Red Army recaptures Kazan

November	End of First World War. Russian Soviet republic declares the Treaty of Brest-Litovsk null and void. Kolchak is proclaimed Supreme Ruler in Omsk. Estonian Soviet republic is announced
December	Committees of the village poor are abolished. Kolchak takes Perm in Urals. Latvian and Lithuanian Soviet republics are announced. Petlyura takes over Ukrainian government

1919

January	System of Politburo and Orgburo is introduced to Bolshevik Party Central Committee. Red Army takes eastern Ukraine. Belorussian Soviet republic is established
February	Quota system of grain requisitioning is formalised. Red Army takes Kiev
March	First Congress of Communist International. Eighth Congress of Russian Communist Party. Short-lived Soviet republics are created in Hungary and Munich. Ukrainian Soviet republic is restored
April	Kolchak's advance is halted
May	Beginning of Denikin's offensive
August	Red Army evacuates Ukraine
October	Yudenich advances towards Petrograd. Denikin is defeated. Then Yudenich is defeated
December	Reds recapture Kiev

1920

January	Allies end blockade of Soviet Russia. Labour armies are introduced
February	Kolchak is executed. Estonian state independence is recognised by the Russian Soviet republic
April	Intensification of military hostility with Poland. Azerbaijani Soviet republic is formed
May	Piłsudski captures Kiev, but is forced to retreat in July
July	Lithuanian state independence is recognised by the Russian Soviet republic
August	Latvian state independence is recognised by the Russian Soviet republic. Poles defeat Red Army at battle of the Vistula
December	Armenian Soviet republic is established

1921

February	Politburo agrees to introduce New Economic Policy. Georgian Soviet republic is formed
March	Kronstadt naval garrison mutinies. Tenth Party Congress confirms New Economic Policy and bans Workers' Opposition and other factions in the party
1922	Genoa Conference. Lenin falls seriously ill. Show trial of Socialist-Revolutionaries. Formal comprehensive system of pre-publication censorship is introduced
1922–23	Ailing Lenin composes his 'political testament'
1923	'Scissors crisis' in state economic management. Left Opposition is formed
1924	Lenin dies. USSR formally comes into existence. Petrograd is renamed Leningrad. Restoration of commercial links with the UK. Stalin, Kamenev and Zinoviev harass Trotski
1925	Leningrad Opposition is created by Kamenev and Zinoviev to oppose Stalin and Bukharin
1925–26	Anti-kulak fiscal measures are introduced
1926	Kamenev, Zinoviev ally with Trotski to form United Opposition against Stalin and Bukharin
1928	Stalin visits Siberia and reintroduces grain requisitioning. Peasant resistance. The First Five-Year Plan begins. Trotski is deported. Kamenev and Zinoviev recant. Shakhty engineers are put on trial. Stalin and Bukharin fall out politically

Index

soldiers: under Imperial
monarchy, 21, 30, 33, 42,
47, 51
under Provisional Government,
43–44, 53–56, 60, 63
under Soviet government, 74,
77, 79, 87
Solovki, 97
South America, 17
south Caucasus, 25, 36, 75
southern Russia, 24, 26, 76, 80
Soviet-Polish War, 88–89
soviets, 31, 33, 43–44, 53, 55–57,
61–64, 67, 69, 74–75, 79,
81–82
see also Sovnarkom,
All-Russian Central Executive
Committee
Soviet Union, *see* USSR
Sovnarkom, 74–83, 98
sown area, *see under* landed
nobility, peasants
Spain, 17
Spartacists, 88
sport, 100
Stalin, I. V., 2, 4–6, 8–9, 16, 36,
87–88, 93, 98, 102–104,
106–107
standard of living, material:
under Imperial monarchy,
15, 18–19, 26, 29, 40, 47–48
under Provisional Government,
53–55, 59–60, 63
under Soviet government, 76,
77, 79, 85–86, 92, 96, 103
State Conference, 68
State Council, 34–35
state monopoly of trade in grain,
59, 79, 91
state ownership in industry:
under Imperial monarchy,
22
under Soviet government, 74,
76, 78, 85, 93–94
steel, 23
steppes, 18
Stockholm Conference, 58

Stolypin, P. A., 33–34, 38
Straits of Dardanelles, 17, 42
street demonstrations, 42, 50–51,
54, 57, 65, 81
strikes, 28–32, 40, 42, 48, 50–51,
59, 77, 89, 94
students, 30
sugar beet, 24, 92
Sunday schools, 37
Supreme Council of the National
Economy, 99
surveyors, 95
Sverdlov, Y. M., 75, 87
Switzerland, 64

Tambov, 91
Tannenberg, battle of, 42
tariffs, 22, 27
taxation, 21, 29, 37, 91–92, 102
direct taxes, 22
indirect taxes, 22
terror: 'individual', 30
mass (Red and White), 71–72,
87–88, 96, 103
Texas, 23
textile industry, 23, 50, 59
timber, 18
Tolstoi, L. N., 35
tractors, 101–103
trade unions: under Imperial
monarchy, 29, 31, 33, 37
under Provisional Government,
43, 61
under Soviet government, 87,
94, 100
transport, 15, 18, 23, 39, 45, 59,
72, 76, 87
Trans-Siberian railway, 23
Trotski, L. D., 4–6, 40, 61, 67,
69–70, 77, 80–81, 83–85,
87–88, 92, 94, 101–102
Trubetskoi, N., 3
Tsaritsyn, 62, 67
Tsereteli, I. G., 57, 61–62, 68
Turkestan, 24
Turkey, 17, 57
see also Ottoman empire